THE

GOD

OF THE

SECOND

CHANCE...

Book of Jonah
Johnny A Palmer Jr.

INTRODUCTION

I do not know about you, but my life has been one gracious second chance from God after another. If I had a half penny for every time the Lord has picked my sorry hide up off the ground, I would be the wealthiest man on the planet. I am truly thankful not only that the Lord has saved me, but has kept me saved for all of these years – and will throughout eternity!

OUTLINE

I. Second Chance is Required. 1:1-16

A. The Chance. 1:1-2
B. The Wrong Choice. 1:3
C. The Chase. 1:4-16

II. Second Chance Received. 1:17-3:10

A. Jonah's Conveyance. 1:17
B. Jonah's Compliance. 2:1-9
C. Jonah's Second Chance. 2:10-3:10

III. Second Chance can be Rejected. 4:1-11

A. Jonah Languished. 4:1-5
B. Jehovah's Lesson. 4:6-11

BACKGROUND TO THE BOOK OF JONAH

Intro:

1. In Basketball one of the most important skills for players to have is the ability to rebound. Rebounds occur because a shot somewhere has been missed. There is no need for a rebound unless something has been missed. If a shot was missed, that means a shot was attempted, but somehow something went wrong in the attempt that caused the shot to be missed, and therefore, we have the need for a rebound. One reason a shot can be missed is that a player was off in their perspective. They may have shot too short, too long, too hard, or too soft. Another reason that shots are missed in basketball games is because the opposing team is in a player's face. It's the job of the opposing team to wave their hands in the shooter's face and obstruct their view. They are supposed to provide a distraction. Sometimes shots are missed because a player is fouled. A foul means that a player has been illegitimately handled, producing an inability for them to make the shot. Any coach will want their player to go for a rebound on their missed shot. In the Bible, there are lots of people who missed shots. Many of God's servants missed their target and had to deal with the consequences of missing their shot. In fact, a study of the Word of God will turn up many people whom God used who were on the rebound.[1]

---

[1] Evans, Tony. Tony Evans' Book of Illustrations: Stories, Quotes, and

2. Jonah missed a golden opportunity to obey God, but by the grace of God, God allowed Jonah to rebound. That same God is our God, and He still allows us to rebound, to have a second chance, to make a U-turn, to do a do-over.

3. The God of the Second Chance.

Trans: Let us begin by looking at the background of the book of Jonah.

First, this is one of the twelve books that we call "The Minor Prophets."

I. FIRST, THE *AUTHOR*.

A. His *Reality*.

This is a real person, in a real historical narrative:

1. Jonah was seen in the historical *Record* (2Kg 14:25).

2. Jewish tradition *Recognized* this book as historical (Josephus, Antiquities IX, 10:2 and the apocryphal Book of Tobit 14:4ff.). Flanigan notes, "Josephus, the Jewish historian, writes but briefly about Jonah but

---

Anecdotes from More Than 30 Years of Preaching and Public Speaking (p. 66). Moody Publishers. Kindle Edition.

follows the ancient Jewish tradition which firmly accepts that the story of Jonah is authentic literal history, not folklore or fable but an integral part of the canon of inspired Scriptures."[2]

3. Christ's *Reference* to Jonah can be seen in Mt 12:39-41; 16:4, and Lk 11:29-32. Jonah's experience in the fish is seen as a sign of Christ's death and resurrection (Mt 12:39-40; 16:4; Lk 11:29-32), and the response of Nineveh to Jonah's preaching was a rebuke to the unbelieving Jews of Christ's day (Mt 12:41; Lk 11:32).

Dr. Tatford comments:

"Our Lord's references to Jonah were quite incompatible with any doubt as to the reliability and authenticity of the book. His statements in Matthew 12:38-42; 16:4; Luke 11:29-32 showed plainly that He accepted the account of Jonah's experiences and the effect of His ministry upon the people of Nineveh. It is clear that He did not regard the book as parabolical or mythological, but as completely historical. He referred to Jonah almost in the same breath as Solomon and the Queen of Sheba, as though all the events which He mentioned were equally authentic."[3]

---

[2] What the Bible Teaches, Ritchie Old Testament Commentaries, Jonah, J. M. Flanigan, p. 479. John Ritchie LTD, Christian Publications.
[3] Ibid.

4. A *Reading* of it indicates that it is a historical account.

Daniel Arnold notes:

The author provides an historical framework for his account. Not only is the prophet mentioned by name, but the book begins like historical accounts do (see Commentary, 1: 1 p. 99). These first elements are very important, because they guide the course of the entire reading. "The reader's initial reaction to the text will determine how he continues to view the narrative. If the opening lines are stylistically in keeping with other historical narratives, it is only natural that he should treat the text as factual.[4]

Years ago in Chicago two homosexuals by the names of Leopold and Loeb were brought to trial for the murder of a young man. Their lawyer was the well-known agonistic defense attorney Clarence Darrow, the man famous for the arguments at the Scopes' trial regarding the teaching of evolution in the public schools of Tennessee. The Chicago trial was a long one, but at last drew to a close and Darrow found himself summing up the evidence. The testimony of one witness had been particularly damaging. So Darrow referred to it, saying, "Why, a person could as easily believe this

---

[4]Arnold, Daniel. Wrestling with God: Bible commentary on the Book of Jonah (p. 76). Unknown. Kindle Edition.

man's testimony as he could believe that the whale swallowed Jonah."

If truth were known the reason why people reject this book as historical is because they reject God and His sovereign power! By the way there were some on the jury that day that did believe the fish had swallowed Jonah and convicted Leopold and Loeb as guilty![5]

The people's problem is not with Jonah and the fish but with the power of God!

O. S. Hawkins notes, "Why should we think it strange that God could prepare a fish to swallow Jonah? If you were in my city today, I would take you to Port Everglades. Docked in that port, you would find a nuclear submarine, a great vessel of human ingenuity and engineering, that can keep persons alive for several months under the sea. If human being's can prepare an iron fish like that, why do some of us have difficulty believing that God who made the world and flung the stars in space could perform a miracle as mundane as preparing a fish for a runaway prophet named Jonah?"[6]

---

[5] An Expositional Commentary – The Minor Prophets, Volume 1: Hosea-Jonah, Paperback ed. (Grand Rapids, MI: Baker Books, 2006), WORDsearch CROSS e-book, 261.
[6] Meeting the God of the Second Chance, Jonah, O. S. Hawkins, p. 13. Loizeaux Brothers, Neptune, New Jersey.

It reminds me of an atheist who was mocking a Christian about Jonah being swallowed by the fish. He said, "How could he live for 3 days in the belly of the fish?" The Christian replied, "I don't know, but when I get to heaven I'm going to ask him about it." The atheist said, "Well, what if he is not there?" He replied, "Then you ask him!"

B. His *Identity*.

He was a prophet (2 Ki. 14:25/Mt. 12:39; 16:4/Lu. 11:29).

He is the author of the book of Jonah – Jon. 1:1.

Henry Morris notes:

The Book of Jonah was almost certainly written originally by the prophet himself. It was written in the third person, but this was a common style of writing, even in autobiographical narratives. No one would have been able to write about his unique experiences except Jonah himself.[7]

Jonah means "dove" and even the meaning of his name brings to mind the idea of a second chance. This word is used in the Noah story in Genesis 8. Noah sends the dove three times to

---

[7] Henry Morris. The Remarkable Journey of Jonah (Kindle Locations 102-103). Master Books. Kindle Edition.

look for land. The first time the dove returns, it failed to find land. So it is given a second chance and succeeds, it comes back with a "plucked-off olive leaf" (Genesis 8: 11). Jonah likewise after failing is given a second chance!

God is the God of the second chance!

The Huffington Post ran a beautiful story about a church in Honolulu called Bluewater Mission. This small church started a restaurant called *Seed*, which gives people a second chance at work and at life. The article focused on a woman named Mary Nelson, who started working at Seed last year. It was only the second job the 53-year-old had ever had. At the age of 14, Nelson's mother committed suicide and she started working on the streets of New York City as a prostitute. Then when she was in her early 50's some Christians at Bluewater Mission persuaded her to leave the streets and try working at Seed. Mary noted that what she makes in a month at Seed, she used to make in one night on the streets. She had it all: new cars, jewelry, travel, nice condos—though, sometimes, beatings, rape and "so much horror" came with the price. "You can't buy what I'm going through right now," she says. "I never thought that I'd be this person I am now."
Recently, Nelson went with her church on a trip to the Philippines to reach out to prostitutes. She told the reporter:

"I want those women to know there's hope. You can change. There are people out there that really want to help and you've got to...believe. Just like you went out there and took a chance on the streets, you've got to take a chance on this as well."[8]

The only one who can really give a second chance, to both the lost and saved, is the Lord Jesus Christ.

We should not forget two things:

One, this should never encourage us to sin.

Two, God does not always give people a second chance (Esau/1 Ki. 13:7-10, 24-26/Num. 20:12).

C. His *Family.*

Son of Amittai – [a- MIT- ih] - derives from the Hebrew word emet, which means truth.

The truth is, the Bible is full of people who were given a second chance.

- Abraham was told to leave his kindred and go to the land that God would show him. He took his kin with him and went

---

[8] Adapted from Carla Herreria, "Restaurant In Hawaii Offers Fresh Start For Former Prostitutes, Convicts, Others Who Need A Hand," The Huffington Post (2-28-15).

to Haran for 5 or 6 years. But God then spoke to him again.

- Moses got ahead of God and killed a man to deliver Israel from Egyptian bondage, and things stalled for some 40 years! But God gave him a second chance at the burning bush.

- Israel repeatedly sinned, cried out to God and was given a second chance – read the book of Judges.

- David committed Adultery and murder, but was given a second chance and died still king of Israel.

- Peter denied the Lord, but was the keynote speaker on the Day of Pentecost.

- John Mark deserted Paul on their missionary trip, but was given another chance from both Barnabas and eventually Paul (2 Tim. 4:11).

Since 2006 a group of people celebrate an important event around the New Year. It's called Good Riddance Day. Participants write down unpleasant, painful, or embarrassing memories from the past year and throw them into an industrial-strength shredder. Or if you prefer, you can also take a sledge hammer and smash your good riddance item, like a cell phone, for instance. The U.S. event is based after a Latin American tradition in which New Year's revelers stuffed dolls with objects representing bad memories before setting them on fire. One of the Good Riddance Day organizers said:

"It really is this need we have, even when the world is crazy, to say, 'You know what? I'm gonna let go of the things that have been dragging me down and going to look forward with a sense of hope and the possibility of change. Either for myself personally or the world.' So this is a chance to detox in a big way."[9]

God has a Good Riddance that really works! When we confess our sin, He is faithful and just to cleanse us from all sin. And we say good riddance to past sin and are given a chance to began a fresh walk with God.

D. His *City*.

Gath Hepher - From Joshua 19: 10-13, we learn that Gath Hepher was located in the territory of Zebulun, in what became the Northern Kingdom following the division of the monarchy. It was located about 3 to 5 miles northeast of Nazareth in Galilee, which made

---

[9] Erin Clarke, "Bad 2016 Memories Smashed at Times Square 'Good Riddance Day,'" Warner Cable News (12-28-16).

the religious leaders complaint that no prophet has risen from Galilee wrong (Jn. 7:52)!

E. His *Popularity*.

In 2 Kings 14:25. Jonah predicted that King Jeroboam II of Israel (783–753 B.C.) would extend the Northern Kingdom's territory almost to the extent of the Davidic kingdom. Jonah immediately became a national hero with a reputation of being a great prophet of God.

F. His observance of God's *Mercy*.

This book is full of the mercy of God:

- Jonah saw it first-hand when God enlarged Israel's boarders in spite of the fact that king Jeroboam II was a wicked king (2 Ki. 14:24).

Not only was the king wicked but the people also, God sent both Hosea and Amos to warn of impending judgment. Because of Israel's stubbornness, the nation would fall under God's chosen instrument of wrath, a Gentile nation from the east. Amos warned that God would send Israel "into exile beyond Damascus" (Amos 5:27). Hosea specifically delineated the ravaging captor as Assyria: "Will not Assyria rule over them because they refuse to repent?" (Hosea 11:5)

- We see the mercy of God in sparing those pagan sailors.
- We see the mercy of God in sparing Jonah from drowning.
- We see the mercy of God in bringing revival to Nineveh.

It is only by God's mercy that any of us is given a second chance, there is not a single one of us that deserves a do-over! We not only do not get what we deserve, which is hell, but by grace, we get what we don't deserve another chance.

It was the first night of camp, and a group of tough kids from the city had hardly unpacked when the leaders received word about a theft. A work crew kid was missing a wallet, $35, and a watch. The next morning, Kirk, the intern from the city, found the empty wallet in his cabin. He immediately called his guys together and hit them with the hard facts:

"Man, you guys did exactly what society expected you to do. You just proved them right. And it's a shame. Now you've got 20 minutes to produce that money and the watch, or we're all going home."

Kirk walked out and shut the door. He could hear the guys shouting at one another and scrambling around inside the cabin. In a moment, the door opened again, and the toughest kid in the crowd presented Kirk with the $35 and the watch. The money was

already spent, but the kids had emptied their pockets and pooled their cash.
When the staff person came to pick up the stolen goods, someone asked, "Who did it?" Kirk replied, "We all did it. We're all guilty. We're in this together." The kids were shocked by Kirk's display of solidarity. Then he shut the cabin door and started to preach:

"Let's talk about grace, grace is getting something you don't deserve. God is going to correct you, but he's going to forgive you. Jesus is going to break you, but he's going to remake you. We all deserve to go home, but we're going to get to stay."

A few nights later, Kirk invited the work crew kid who had been robbed to come to his cabin and to share his own experience of God's grace with the guys. After the young man left that night, Kirk said:

"Now I'm going to say a prayer, and if any of you want to pray with me and give your lives to God, then just do it." By the end of the prayer, 17 baritone voices had cried out to Jesus Christ.[10]

II. FURTHERMORE, THE *APPROXIMATE* DATE.

760 B.C.

---

[10] Denny Rydberg, president of Young Life, from October 1999 ministry letter.

III. THIRD, THE *ASSESSMENT* OF THE SITUATION.

"Jonah was a contemporary of Jeroboam II of Israel (782-753 B.C.) who ministered after the time of Elisha and just before the time of Amos and Hosea. Israel was enjoying a period of resurgence and prosperity, and nationalistic fervor was probably high. Assyria, a nation which had achieved a near-legendary reputation for cruelty, was in mild decline during these years, but it remained a threat. The repentance of Nineveh probably occurred in the reign of Ashurdan III (773-755 B.C)."[11]

IV. FOURTH, THE *AIM* OF THE BOOK.

A. To reveal God's *Mercy.*

B. To reveal God's powerful *Sovereignty.*

1. The resting of the ragging sea (1:15)
2. The rescuing of Jonah by the appointment of a fish (1:17)
3. The releasing of Jonah from the fish to the land (2:10)
4. The repentance of Nineveh (3)
5. The remarkable appointments of the plant, worm, and east wind (4:6-8).

---

[11] Nelson's Complete Book of Bible Maps & Charts, Thomas Nelson Publishers, p. 255.

G. Campbell Morgan had it right, "Men have been looking so long at the great fish they have failed to see the great God!"

C. To reveal the *Universality* of God's salvation.

God is not just interested in saving Jews but Gentiles as well.

V. AN *ACCEPTABLE* OUTLINE.

I. Second Chance is *Required.* Chp. 1-2
II. Second Chance is *Received*. Chp. 3
III. Second Chance can be *Rejected.* Chp. 4
-Johnny A Palmer Jr.

There are many other good outlines:

Jonah's Disobedience [in a Ship]. Chp. 1
Jonah's Distress [in a Sea Creature]. Chp. 2
Jonah's Declaration [in a big City]. Chp. 3
Jonah's Displeasure [on the Side of a hill]. Chp. 4 -Charles Ryrie

I. Running from God.
II. Running to God.
III. Running with God.
IV. Running ahead of God.
-Derward William Deere

Focus:
First Commission of Jonah. Chps. 1-2
Second Commission of Jonah. Chps. 3-4

Topic:
God's Mercy upon Jonah. Chps. 1-2
God's Mercy upon Nineveh. Chps. 3-4

Location:
The Great Sea. Chps. 1-2
The Great City. Chps. 3-4
-Nelson's Complete Book of Bible Maps and Charts

I. Running from God's Will. Chp. 1
II. Submitting to God's Will. Chp. 2
III. Fulfilling God's Will. Chp. 3.
IV. Questioning God's Will. Chp. 4
-John MacArthur

Con:

1. This is a great book because sooner or later we all need a Second Chance, a do-over, to rebound.

2. We are not talking about two chances when we talk of another chance. We mean another chance, like a millionth chance and then some!

3. The actor Bill Murray claimed that a work of art once saved his life. He was in Chicago for his first experience as an actor. Murray said:

"[My performance] was so bad that I just walked out afterward and onto the street. I kept walking for a couple of hours. Then I realized that I walked in the wrong direction and not in just the wrong direction from where I lived, but in the desire to stay alive."

He headed for Lake Michigan as he contemplated taking his own life. Murray continued:

I thought, "If I'm going to die, I might as well go over toward the lake and float a bit." So, I walked toward the lake and reached Michigan Avenue and started walking north. Somehow I ended up in front of the Art Institute and walked inside. There was a painting of a [simple peasant] woman working in a field with a sunrise behind her. I always loved that painting. I saw it that night and said, "Look, there's a girl without a whole lot of prospects, but the sun's coming up and she's got another chance at it." I said, "I'm a person, too, and will get another chance every single day." After gazing at the painting, Murray decided to live.[12]

22 The LORD'S lovingkindnesses indeed never cease, For His compassions never fail. 23 *They are new every morning; Great is Your faithfulness.* Lamentations 3:22-23 (NASB)

Chapter One
THE SECOND CHANCE IS REQUIRED

---

[12] Cindy Pearlman, "The Art Institute moment that saved Bill Murray's career," Chicago Sun Times (10-13-17)

Jonah 1:1-16

The Chance

Intro:

1. I never did very well in school, I hated being called to the blackboard and having to work out some problem. Usually several people were up there on the blackboard working out a problem. One of the things that saved my hide was the eraser! I would get a quick glance at the person next to me, and then erase what I had written and put his answer up there. I used it profusely, I erased mistake after mistake with that eraser. It gave me a second change to get it right.

2. As a Christian, I have also made mistake after mistake, it sounds better than sin after sin. But I would not be standing behind this pulpit today if it were not for the God of the Second Chance who not only wipes out our sin with His blood, but gives us another chance to get it right.

3. The Second Chance is Required – because of our many failures.

I. FIRST, THE SECOND CHANCE IS *REQUIRED*.

A. First, the *Chance*. 1:1-2

1. It is *Continual*.

"And it was..." – this is how it begins in the original.

J. M. Flanigan notes:

"The little word "Now" or :And: as many translations prefer, with which the book begins...In Hebrew, as in any language, it is a conjunction, a joining word which implies and preserves continuity with what has gone before. Appearing in the opening verses of Exodus, Leviticus and Numbers, it thereby joins the first four books of Moses, as it does also the books of Joshua, Judges, Ruth, and the books of the kings. Ezra and Esther commence in the same way, as does the prophecy of Ezekiel. Here Jonah...unites his prophecy with that of others and maintains the uniformity of the inspired writings." [What the Bible teaches, Richie Old Testament Commentaries, Jonah p. 503].
The Bible is not just a bunch of scattered writings, but, there is a definite unity of mind from Genesis to Revelation! James M. Boice notes:
A sixth reason for regarding the Bible as the revealed Word of God is the extraordinary unity of the book...The Bible is composed of sixty-six parts, or books, written over a period of approximately fifteen hundred years (from about 1450 B.C. to about A.D. 90) by over

forty different people. These people were not alike. They came from various levels of society and from diverse backgrounds. Some were kings. Others were statesmen, priests, prophets, a tax collector, a physician, a tentmaker, fishermen. If asked about any subject at all, they would have had views as diverse as the opinions of people living today. Yet together they produced a volume that is a marvelous unity in its doctrine, historical viewpoints, ethics and expectations. It is, in short, a single story of divine redemption begun in Israel, centered in Jesus Christ and culminating at the end of history. The nature of this unity is important... What can account for this unity? There is only one way of accounting for it: behind the efforts of the more than forty human authors is the one perfect, sovereign and guiding mind of God.[13]

R. A. Torrey notes:

It is not a superficial unity, but a profound unity. On the surface, we often find apparent discrepancy and disagreement, but, as we study, the apparent discrepancy and disagreement disappear, and the deep underlying unity appears. The more deeply we study, the more complete do we find the unity to be. The unity is also an organic one—that is, it is not the unity of a dead thing, like a stone,

---

[13] James M. Boice, Foundations of the Christian Faith: A Comprehensive & Readable Theology, (Downers Grove, IL: InterVarsity Press, 1986), WORDsearch CROSS e-book, 58-59.

but of a living thing, like a plant. In the early books of the Bible we have the germinant thought; as we go on we have the plant, and further on the bud, and then the blossom, and then the ripened fruit. In Revelation we find the ripened fruit of Genesis.[14]

Geoff Wood writes that a stained glass illustrates the importance of the Old Testament:

High over the portals within the south transept of the 800-year-old cathedral of Chartres in France spreads a great Rose window, forty feet in diameter. At its center sits Christ, while immediately around him orbit eight angels and symbols for the four evangelists, each enclosed within a circle of stained glass-and beyond them orbit the 24 elders of the book of Revelation, each also within its own bejeweled circle—for a total of 36 orbiting circles of blue, red, gold, purple, and white! Enough to make your head spin. Nor is that gigantic wheel of color the only thing to enchant you in that soaring wing of the cathedral, because below it rise five more long and narrow windows, the central one featuring Mary, while the other four show images of the evangelists, Luke and Matthew, John, and Mark-in that sequence. Now if you look closely at the windows for the four gospel writers, you'll notice something

---

[14] R. A. Torrey, The Bible and Its Christ (New York: Fleming H. Revell, 1904-6), p. 26.

amusing. All four, appearing almost boyish in size, sits on the shoulders of a tall prophet of the Old Testament: Luke on the shoulders of Jeremiah, Matthew on Isaiah's, John on Ezekiel's, and Mark on Daniel's. The four major voices of the New Testament ride piggyback on the four major voices of the Old—just the way a dad might lift a small child on his shoulders. Why would those artists do something as playful as that? Well, it wasn't playful. They wanted to make a serious point, namely that the gospels build on the wisdom and vision of the Old Testament.[15]

2. It was *Audible*.

a. We have the *Logos*.

[1] *The word of the LORD...saying* – in the LXX the Greek translation of the Old Testament, "word" is the Greek Logos. This word occurs 917 times in the O.T., and 330 times in the N.T. I assume this was audible. This was common in the Old Testament. The "word of the Lord" is said to have come to Abraham, Nathan, David, Solomon, Jehu, Elijah, Isaiah, Haggai, Zechariah, etc. Today we have something even greater; we have the full and final written Word of God. He is still speaking, not audibly, but speaking by His Spirit through His Written Word. O. S. Hawkins notes, "This

---

[15] Adapted from Geoff Wood, Living the Lectionary Year C, (Liturgy Training Publications, 2007), page 101.

was not the word of man; it was "the word of the Lord." Men do not call us; it is God who calls us. Jonah had a God who spoke to him…He did not have the word of God, the final complete written revelation, as we do today…the same God who spoke to the prophets in the past now speaks to us directly by the Holy Spirit through His Word…Has the word of the Lord come to you this week? If not, you have not spent time with Him."[16]

1 God, after He spoke long ago to the fathers in the prophets in many portions and in many ways, 2 in these last days has spoken to us in His Son, whom He appointed heir of all things, through whom also He made the world. Hebrews 1:1-2

7 Therefore, just as the Holy Spirit says, "TODAY IF YOU HEAR HIS VOICE, 8 DO NOT HARDEN YOUR HEARTS AS WHEN THEY PROVOKED ME, AS IN THE DAY OF TRIAL IN THE WILDERNESS, Hebrews 3:7-8

As one put it:

I've imagined this scene in my head: I'm playing baseball with Jesus. The stands are full of fans, but out there on the field it's just him and me. I'm the pitcher. Jesus is the catcher, behind home plate. He settles into his crouch,

---

[16] Meeting the God of the Second Chance, Jonah, O.S. Hawkins, pp. 22-23. Loizeaux Brothers Neptune, New Jersey.

ready to play, and *I* look for his signals—simple commands. What pitch will he want me to throw? I wait in anticipation, but also with one eye on the crowd. What will they think of me? He signals a fastball. I think for a moment and shake my head—no, not a fastball.
Next he signals a slider. This time I look toward my teammates in the dugout for guidance. Then I glance up at the fans. No, I'm not comfortable with that one either.
He gives me yet a third signal. No, not today, thank you! Then I imagine Jesus silently and slowly withdrawing his signaling hand back into his mitt. There's a deep disappointment in his eyes. He's decided to let me throw whatever I want. So I do—and then I wonder why there's just no team spirit anymore! Has Jesus stopped giving you signals?
I doubt it. He never stops speaking to his children. Is there a signal God's been trying to give you, even as you read this sentence, that you've ignored because you just don't want to obey?[17]

Actually, the worst thing that could happen is for God to remove his Word from this Nation.

¹¹ "Behold, days are coming," declares the Lord GOD, "When I will send a famine on the land, Not a famine for bread or a thirst for water, But rather for hearing the words of the

---

[17] Clare de Graff, The 10-Second Rule (Howard Books, 2013), pp. 52-53.

LORD. [12] "People will stagger from sea to sea And from the north even to the east; They will go to and fro to seek the word of the LORD, But they will not find *it.* Amos 8:11-12 (NASB)

This nation has the Word of God, but I am not sure most people are listening to it. J. Vernon McGee observes:

Here is a most unusual famine. God had given them His Word, and they had rejected it. They had despised it and turned aside from it. Now God tells that the day is coming when they will no longer have the privilege of hearing His Word. God tells any church or any nation that if they will not hear His Word after He has given it to them, He will withdraw it from them. I think we can see this happening in America. There has been a rejection of the Word of God. The churches have turned to liberalism, and the Word of God is no longer preached. There has come a famine of the Word of God. So many of the formerly great churches of this country, the great downtown churches, have turned from the Word of God... Actually, very little of the Word of God is getting out in this land today. There is a Gideon Bible in every room in every hotel and motel in this country. Nearly everyone owns a Bible. But who is studying it? Who is reading it? Who is believing it? I think we are beginning to see the famine of the Word of God in this country.[18]

b. We have the *LORD*.

The word "LORD", the Hebrew word Jehovah or Yahweh, speaks of the eternal, self-existent One. It appears 26 times in this little book. Throughout Scripture, the Lord is known by several titles which reveals His work with mankind.

- **Jehovah-jireh=** The Lord our Provider
- **Jehovah-rapha=** The Lord our Healer
- **Jehovah-nissi=** The Lord our Banner
- **Jehovah-shalom=** The Lord our Peace
- **Jehovah-ra-ah=** The Lord our Shepherd
- **Jehovah-tsidkenu=** The Lord our Righteousness

Briefly let's look at Yahweh in this little book:

- **He Communicates with us.** 1:1; 3:1, 3; 4:4.

God is always communicating with us! He speaks to us primarily today through His Written Word, by the Holy Spirit. We live in a dark, sinful world, and it is by the Word of God that God speaks to us.

[19] *So we have the prophetic word made more sure, to which you do well to pay attention as to a lamp shining in a dark place, until the day*

---

[18] J. Vernon McGee, *Thru The Bible with J. Vernon McGee*, (Nashville, TN: Thomas Nelson, 1983), WORD*search* CROSS e-book, Under: "Chapter 8".

dawns and the morning star arises in your hearts. 2 Peter 1:19

John Philips notes:

So Peter comes to the point: "We have also a more sure word of prophecy." Even such authentic and awesome voices and visions as characterized the Mount of Transfiguration have their place, no doubt, but they cannot be compared with the Word of God, with that "more sure word of prophecy." Many people lightly set aside the Word of God in favor of visions of dubious sorts and voices of unknown origin. It is a dangerous practice. Voices and visions can originate from satanic and demonic sources. Drugs can induce them. False religions and various cults of Christendom have frequently been based on such deceptive phenomena. Occult religions are motivated by satanic voices and spurious visions. Legions of lying spirits in the unseen world are clamoring to be heard and heeded, and millions of deluded people, who will not have the Bible at any price, eagerly embrace phenomena emanating from the Deceiver himself. No! We have "a more sure word of prophecy," God's written Word, the Bible. We need nothing else.[19]

Isn't it exciting to think that The LORD God has something to say specifically to us!

---

[19] John Phillips, The John Phillips Commentary Series – Exploring the Epistles of Peter: An Expository Commentary, (Grand Rapids, MI: Kregel Publications, 2005), WORDsearch CROSS e-book, 249-250.

Seth Godin tell about his friend Jacqueline, who tells the story, of how UNICEF spent a fortune creating posters to promote the idea of child vaccination to the mothers of Rwanda. She said: "The posters were gorgeous—photographs with women and children with simple messages written in Kinyarwandan (the local language), about the importance of vaccinating every child. They were perfect, except for the fact with a female illiteracy rate exceeding 70 percent, words written in perfect Kinyarwandan made little difference." Jacqueline noticed that the way messages spread in Rwanda was by song. One group of women would sing a song for other women, both as a way of spreading ideas and as a gift. No song, no message. Your tribe communicates. They probably don't do it the way you would; they don't do it as efficiently as you might like, but they communicate. The challenge for the leader is to help your tribe sing, whatever form that song takes.[20]

The point is, God uses the Bible, but He has a way of communicating that Bible in a way that is easy for us to understand. I think that is why He allows so many translations of the Bible. Most of them say the same thing, but some translations communicate to us in ways other translations do not. I suppose that is why Satan comes along and tries to discredit any

---

[20] Seth Godin, Tribes (Portfolio, 2008), page 124; submitted by Timothy Liu, Virginia Beach, Virginia.

translation but the KJV. That's silly! Of course, that is not to discredit the KJV either. I have known many godly men whom God' speaks to through that version. Do not be afraid to experiment. Find a translation that uses words that communicate best to you, I prefer the NAS, others the NIV. Just make sure you get a good solid translation that reflects the original languages. A popular one today seems to be the ESV.

- **He can be *Consciously* known.** 1:3, 10

Notice he is seeking to flee "from the presence of the Lord." Obviously one cannot flee from the omnipresence of the Lord (Psa. 139:7-12). But there is a conscious, manifested presence of God (Jn. 14:21/2 Cor. 4:7-11/Ja. 4:8/etc.). Spurgeon understood this precious truth, he wrote, "I know what some would say. They would cry, "Nonsense, we believe religion is a good thing, but as to these *manifestations* we do not believe in them!" Very well, the Scripture says, "He does not manifest Himself unto the world...[If you are a believer] you must know something of it, if not much, otherwise you have not gone far on your spiritual course."[21]

---

[21] Spiritual Survivor Man, Johnny A Palmer Jr. Redemption Press, p. 17. 2014.

The sad thing is that if Jonah had obeyed the LORD, His presence would have gone with Jonah to Nineveh.

- **He is the One who is in *Control*.** 1:4, 14b, 17; 4:6.

God is calling the shots, we are little shots that most of the time ought to be shot! Rus Reavens notes:

God's will is supreme, and is not subject to the dictates of another. No one compels God to do something that He does not will to do. He doesn't answer to anyone… He chooses to do so according to His own will. Jonah was not knocking on the door of heaven begging to hear some word from God… It happened because God chose for it to happen and took the initiative… Once you've read the whole story, you will know that Jonah does not appear to be a likely candidate for the ministry. But then again, who is? If God didn't use imperfect people, there would be no people at all for God to use… God is sovereign, always taking the initiative, and we are always in the position of reacting or responding to what He says and does… When we come up against it, we are forced to recognize that we are not in control of our own little universes, and we do not like that idea… We are born believing the lie of our own sovereignty, but God will not let us believe it forever… We are limited, finite creatures. He is infinite and unlimited. We see in these verses that God is not limited by time. He is eternal. He has always existed, and always will.[22]

Pastor Daniel Schreiner from Portland, Oregon received the following marketing piece from a local fitness gym. It was called "The Year of You." [The New Year] is right around the corner and you're either going to own the year OR the year is going to own you. It's 100% your choice. It's in your hands. That's the first thing. Simply by taking all of the responsibility and putting it on your shoulders you become empowered. Next, you take that feeling of empowerment. Of invincibility. The feeling you can run through a wall ... and you take action. You take action like you've never taken action before. You become prolific. You become consistent. And you let no obstacle stand in your way ... no matter what. No more pity parties. No more whining about anything. YOU are in control. YOU.[23]

That lie is both arrogant and ignorant! The reality is that God is the one in control!

[13] ...God, who is the blessed controller of all things, the king over all kings and the master of all masters. 1 Timothy 6:15 (Phillips NT)

---

[22] Reaves, Russ. Jonah: An Expository Commentary (Kindle Location 767). . Kindle Edition.
[23] Daniel Schreiner, Sermon "The Supremacy of God," PreachingToday.com.

He is in control not only of the Rulers (1 Chron. 29:12/Dan. 4) but of even something as significant as the death of sparrow.

> ²⁹ Two sparrows cost only a penny, but not even one of them can die without your Father's knowing it. Matthew 10:29 (NCV)

It is God, not us, who will decide the events of this coming year!

- **There should be *Conformity* to His will**. 1:9a, 16

Feared the LORD - The verb אָרֵי (yare') has a broad range of meanings, including "to fear, to worship, to revere, to respect" (BDB 431 s.v.). When God is the object, it normally means "to fear" (leading to obedience; BDB 431 s.v. 1) or "to worship" (= to stand in awe of; BDB 431 s.v. 2). Because the fear of God leads to wisdom and obedience, that is probably not the sense here. Instead Jonah professes to be a loyal Yahwist – in contrast to the pagan Phoenician sailors who worshiped false gods, he worshiped the one true God. Unfortunately his worship of the LORD lacked the necessary moral prerequisite.[24]

---

[24] Biblical Studies Press. NET Bible First Edition (with notes) (Kindle Locations 162741-162746). Biblical Studies Press. Kindle Edition.

Our part in relating to the LORD should be radical, unquestioning obedience. See 2 Cor. 10:5/ 1 Pet. 1:14-15

Adrian Rogers shared this, "I had a privilege...years ago...to spend a day in prayer with Dr. Billy Graham and some other men. We met in a hotel room in Dallas for the purpose of spending a day in prayer, just sharing and seeking the face of the Lord. And as we were sitting around a table sharing Billy Graham said something that I shall never forget. He looked around at the rest of us and said gentlemen, I long to be holy. I want to be a holy man. Pray for me, that I will be holy."[25]

That is how we need to relate to Yahweh, with a deep abiding desire to be engaged in holy obedience.

- **He is the *Creator*.** 1:9b

We need to realize that God is God! He is eternal we are created at a point in time; He is self-existent, we exist only because He chose to create us. Isa. 42:5/Rev. 4:11.
We can commit both our life and eternity to One who has created and sustains the universe. William Shakespeare, wrote in his will: "I commend my soul into the hands of God, my Creator, hoping and assuredly

---

[25] Adrian Rogers, *The Adrian Rogers Legacy Collection – Sermons*, (North Palm Beach, FL: Adrian Rogers Foundation, 2011), WORD*search* CROSS e-book, Under: "The Highway to Holiness".

believing, through the merits of Jesus Christ my Savior to be made partaker of Life everlasting."[26]

What we long for is to know the One who is responsible for our being and well-being. Years ago, there was an episode of the original TV series Star Trek. The story involved a Voyager spacecraft sent out from Earth through the solar system, and it had disappeared for hundreds of years.
Somehow it collected unto itself all kinds of other equipment and technology and intelligence. Then it headed back to Earth, and the whole planet was in terror of this enormously powerful thing coming right at them. What was it going to do? Was it going to destroy the world?
Well, of course, Captain Kirk was dispatched to save the day. When he finally encountered this gigantic apparatus and was able to communicate with it, he found that what it wanted was not to destroy the world but to know the world's creator. It also wanted to be joined to its creator.[27]

The truth is, that's what we desire above all else—to know God, the Creator, and be united with Him.

---

[26] Kennedy, D. James. Why I Believe (p. 112). Thomas Nelson. Kindle Edition.
[27] Kennedy, Dr D. James. The Presence of a Hidden God: Evidence for the God of the Bible (p. 34). The Crown Publishing Group. Kindle Edition.

- **He can be *Called upon* in prayer.**
  1:14; 2:1; 4:2-3.

What a wonderful thing prayer is! It says we can actually get in contact with the almighty God! It is better than having a hot line to the president of the United States or anyone else. And it is no gimmick but a real connection to God Himself. In March of 2009, Dutch artist Johan van der Dong decided God needed a telephone number. So, he got him one. A cell phone number to be exact—to show that God was "available anywhere and anytime." Dong said:

"In earlier times you would go to a church to say a prayer, and now [this is an] opportunity to just make a phone call and say your prayer in a modern way."

It seems a lot of people appreciate the opportunity Dong has afforded them with his "divine hotline." Within one week, over 1,000 people left God a message.
Yet when you made the call you heard:
"This is the voice of God. I am not able to speak to you at the moment, but please leave a message." That doesn't exactly convey the idea of a God who is "available anywhere and anytime," does it? To make matters worse, Dong plans on keeping the line open for just six months. Dong has really only managed to connect people to an altogether disconnected

God.[28] Truth is, if we come to our Father through His Son, we will find Him available anywhere and anytime and you don't even need a cell phone!

- **He *Cares* about us.** 2:2, 6-7; 4:10.

God is concerned about the storms that we are going through. See, Lu. 15:20/Heb. 5:2. He cares about Jonah, those sailors, those vile Ninevites, even people that the rest of us have no compassion for at all. A Hasidic story tells of a great celebration in heaven after the Israelites are delivered from the Egyptians at the Red Sea and the Egyptian armies are drowned. The angels are cheering and dancing. Everyone in heaven is full of joy.
Then one of the angels asks the archangel Michael, "Where is God? Why isn't God here celebrating?"
Michael answers, "God is not here because He is off by Himself weeping. You see, many thousands were drowned today."[29]

- **He *Converts*.** 2:9

The word convert means to change – the LORD is in the business of changing things whether

---

[28] Brian Lowery, managing editor, PreachingToday.com; sources: Associated Press, "Dutch leave messages on God phone," www.newsvote.bbc.co.uk (3-7-09), and Reuters, "Leave God a message at his Dutch answering service," www.reuters.com (3-2-09).
[29] Tony Campolo, Let Me Tell You a Story (Word, 2000); submitted by Debi Zahn; Sandwich, Illinois.

physically or spiritually. We cannot change the human heart or circumstances or little else. He can save, deliver, and take life in a new direction.

Trans: The LORD is all we really need in time and eternity, He Communicates; can be known Consciously; is in Control; we can be in Conformity to His will; should be worshipped as the Creator; Called upon; He Cares and Converts! Yet often we neglect God for the worthless things of this world. Paul Tripp shares this about his son:

My wife and I would go out when he was a little guy to buy what we thought was the [perfect] gift. He would tear open the gift, and he'd end up playing with the box. It drove us crazy. We decided on Christmas that we were going to find…the gift of gifts that he would not be able to resist. We shopped and shopped. We found the gift. We were so excited.
We were much more excited at that moment when the gift came out from under the tree and he was about to unwrap it—much more excited than he would have ever been.
He ripped open the gift like a little boy would…and, actually got out this toy and began to play with it. I had a feeling of such victory. I went into the kitchen to get something to drink, was in there for a few minutes, and came out and he was sitting in the box. I couldn't believe it. Then he concluded with this:

If you're one of God's children, you have been given the most awesome gift that could ever be given. It's gorgeous from every perspective. It's a gift of such grandeur that it's hard to wrap human vocabulary around it and explain it. It's beautiful from every vista...It's the gift that every human being needs. It's a gift that in all of your work and all of your effort and all of your achievement you couldn't have ever earned; you could have never deserved; you could have never achieved. It is absolutely without question the gift of gifts. It's the gift of the grace of the Lord Jesus Christ, [but] I am deeply persuaded in the face of this gift, there are many Christians who are content to play with the box.[30]

3. It was *Personal*.

came to Jonah the son of Amittai saying, - we looked at this in the Introduction. Remember the word Jonah means "dove" and we looked at the fact that it is used in Gen. 8, where Noah sent out the dove, who at first failed, but then, given a *Second Chance*, was sent out again. We could also add:

- It is a known to be a *Sad* bird, it often laments an apt description of Jonah in chp. 4

---

[30] Paul Tripp, from the sermon "Playing with the Box," Gospel Coalition; submitted by Van Morris, Mt. Washington, Kentucky.

¹⁴ "Like a swallow, like a crane, so I twitter; I moan like a dove; My eyes look wistfully to the heights; O Lord, I am oppressed, be my security. Isaiah 38:14 (NASB)

¹¹ All of us growl like bears, And moan sadly like doves; We hope for justice, but there is none, For salvation, *but* it is far from us. Isaiah 59:11 (NASB)

- It was also a bird of *Sacrifice*, which Jonah was willing to do to save the sailors.

⁷ 'But if he cannot afford a lamb, then he shall bring to the LORD his guilt offering for that in which he has sinned, two turtledoves or two young pigeons, one for a sin offering and the other for a burnt offering. Leviticus 5:7 (NASB)

- The Psalmist wanted to be a dove, to fly away so as to be *Spared* the terrors of death as Jonah wanted to be spared the terrors of Nineveh.

⁴ My heart is in anguish within me, And the terrors of death have fallen upon me. ⁵ Fear and trembling come upon me, And horror has overwhelmed me. ⁶ I said, "Oh, that I had wings like a dove! I would fly away and be at rest. Psalm 55:4-6 (NASB)

Trans: Well, I am grateful for those erasers, which wiped away my mistakes those many years ago; but even more grateful, as Jonah was that the LORD He knew not only gave His word once, but a Second time after he blew it the first time (3:1).

Christian author Michael Scrogin writes:
We have Halls of Fame all over this country. There's one in Canton, Ohio, for football; one in Springfield, Massachusetts, for basketball; there's one in Cooperstown, New York, for baseball. We have a Halls of Fame for all sorts of sports, and we're forever electing aging athletes to these institutions. Speeches are made in their honor as we give them awards. If it were up to me to make the decisions, I would have a different sort of Hall of Fame. I would have a Hall of Fame of those who have given and those who have received Second and third and 13th CHANCES. This hall would be huge and it would be filled mostly with the names of those who had made it against all odds. I would have a section dedicated especially to those who had been arrested or imprisoned and who later, when they were released, straightened out their lives and didn't go back. I would set aside an entire wall for recovering alcoholics, who'd been up against a devastating disease, who'd hit bottom, but who'd climbed back out. I'd set aside one whole building for teenagers because every teenager needs at least 100 second chances.[31]

I don't know if at the Bema the Lord will be giving out Second Chance awards. If they have such a Hall of Fame for those given a trillion second chances – I'll be in it! At the top of the list, just above, people like Jonah.

In November 2004, 45-year-old Victoria Ruvolo was heading home in Lake Ronkonkoma, New York, after hearing her 14-year-old niece sing at a school recital. At the same time, 19-year-old Ryan Cushing was out joyriding with a group of friends, who had just finished a spending spree at a nearby supermarket— with a stolen credit card. One of the items they bought was a large frozen turkey. As Victoria's car passed Cushing's— he was in the back seat— the teen threw the turkey into oncoming traffic. The 20-pound bird crashed through Victoria's windshield and struck her in the face. The teens didn't stop, and they didn't call 911. Victoria had a passenger who called emergency services, and she was rushed to Stony Brook University Hospital. She was put into a medically induced coma and went through a 10-hour operation to save her from dying. She was kept in the coma for two weeks, and stayed in the hospital for months after that, as doctors reconstructed her shattered face and she went through painful rehabilitation. The doctors said it was miraculous that she survived the ordeal at all.[32]

---

[31] PRACTICAL GUIDE TO CHRISTIAN LIVING by Michael Scrogin, p. 42.

I think Ryan must have had some Assyrian blood in him, that was the type of brutality that they loved to engage in. Who could have anything but contempt for such a vile person – we should, and God does!

We continue on with our study in Jonah, we are looking at his Chance, his opportunity for ministry. We saw related to the book that it is Continual, the Message to Jonah was Audible, Personal, and now we continue on.

4. The Message was *Simple*.

2 *"Arise, go –*

"Arise" is not uncommon in Scripture:

- Jacob—Arise and return to thy kindred.
- Joshua—Arise, and go over this Jordan.
- Gideon—Arise, and get down to the host of Midianites. I have delivered them into your hand.
- Samuel—Arise and anoint Saul.
- Elijah—Arise and go to Zarephath. A widow will care for thee.

God's message to us is just as simple....
"Arise!" Go do what I asked you to do.

---

[32] Bathroom Readers' Institute. Uncle John's Bathroom Reader Tales to Inspire (Uncle John's Bathroom Readers) (Kindle Locations 510-514). Portable Press. Kindle Edition.

5. It was humanly *Impossible*.

a. The Recognizing of our Nineveh.

Frankly most people turn this into an unfair guilt trip!

- It is not about going but doing God's will. It is often just as hard to stay, as it is to go. Many times God has told me to stay when I really wanted to go – anywhere!

- It is not saying that everybody is supposed to be a prophet or an evangelist out publically preaching the gospel. God has given different people different gifts. While we all should share the gospel with the lost, we are not all evangelists.

- It is not a demand for all to go to the mission field. Again not everybody is called to go cross-culturally. We can all pray for missionaries, support them, but that does not mean we are all called to be one on foreign soil.

- Again, I am not saying we should not share the gospel, or rejoice with those called to the mission field. I am saying we can make the Bible say anything we want it to. It is better to let it speak for itself. No add-ons, no personal comments, no misapplications. Your

Nineveh is the ministry that God has given you. How do you know where God has called you to minister? As we have already pointed out we find God's will in the Word of God.

b. The Resisting of God's will.

Tarshish represents our rebellion, our refusing to do what God has called us to do. More about this later.

It's the Texas Rangers' locker room on an August, 1997 afternoon. Star relief pitcher and passionate Christian John Wetteland is flipping through his Bible, talking about why he isn't worried about his religious fervor fitting in with the Rangers' club house.
" ' That would be like Noah asking God—not Noah. What's his name? Went to Nineveh!'
" ' Simsy!' Wetteland yells, startling reserve outfielder Mike Simms, who is watching TV. 'Who refused to go to Nineveh?' Simms stares back blankly." ' Jonah!' Wetteland, the former Yankee, hollers, suddenly remembering and very pleased. 'It would be like Jonah saying to God, "Well, how many people are in Nineveh that are gonna listen to my message that I have from you?" Of course, Jonah decided to go 180 degrees the opposite direction—and you know the rest of the story; he gets barfed up on the beach at Nineveh. When God directs you somewhere, you just go.'"[33]

c. His possible Reasoning for not going.

- He knew his life might be in *Jeopardy*. He was afraid they would kill him. That fear was understandable! Archaeologists have actually discovered monuments that were built by various individuals to their atrocities. Here are some of them:

One of those monuments says, "I cut the limbs off the officers who rebelled."

Another monument states, "Within the border of my own land, I flayed and spread their skins upon the walls."

Another cruel Ninevite wrote, "I cut off their hands and their fingers, and from others I cut off their noses and ears and fingers. For many of them, I put out their eyes."[34]

The historical records of the ancient world describe how Assyria's military would tear off the lips and hands of their victims, skin them alive, and amass piles of their victims' skulls as monuments to their own greatness... One Assyrian king boasted that he had flayed the

---

[33] *6,000 Plus Illustrations for Communicating Biblical Truths*, (Omaha, Nebraska: Christianity Today, 1997), WORD*search* CROSS e-book, Under: "Witnessing".

[34] Laurie, Greg. A Fresh Look At the Book of Jonah: The hard to swallow truth about disobedience (Kindle Locations 117-118). Allen David Books/Kerygma Inc. Kindle Edition.

skin from many nobles, and built towers with decapitated skulls, and hung others from the trees. Boys and girls were burned alive. The king himself claims to have cut off arms and hands, noses, ears, and other extremities, and gouged out eyes.[35]

Fear often keeps us from obeying God. In 1996 two military strategists, Harlan Uliman and James Wade, started advocating a more focused approach to war. Uliman and Wade argued for engaging the enemy with an overwhelming show of force that will destroy "the adversary's will to resist before, during, and after battle." They titled their book *Shock and Awe*. Shortly before the first Iraq War, Uliman described what would happen with this Shock and Awe approach: "You're sitting in Baghdad and all of a sudden you're the general and 30 of your division headquarters have been wiped out. You also take the city down. By that I mean you get rid of their power, water. In 2,3,4,5 days they are physically, emotionally and psychologically exhausted."[36]

I think Jonah felt Shock and Awe about entering Nineveh. It is not uncommon for God's servant to face overwhelming odds and feel fearful. Moses was afraid because he had

---

[35] Reaves, Russ. Jonah: An Expository Commentary (Kindle Locations 852-854). . Kindle Edition.
[36] Matt Woodley, editor, PreachingToday.com; source: Brian Blount, Invasion Of The Dead, (Westminster John Knox Press, 2014), pages 90-91

trouble speaking (Ex. 3:11-); Jeremiah was afraid because he was just a youth (Jer. 1:); Gideon was afraid of the Midianites (Jud. 6:11-16); David was uneasy as he looked Goliath straight in the knee cap (1 Sam. 17:41-).

- **It would be *Just* Jonah!**

Billy Graham always had Cliff Barrows and George Beverly Shea by his side! Daniel went into captivity in Babylon, but he had his three Hebrew friends with him. Even Moses was given Aaron as he confronted Egypt. Jonah had no song leader, crusade team, nothing but himself. It was one thing to deliver a message, like Nahum did from a distance, but to actually go there alone was another thing. [PS: As I write this news of Billy Graham's departure to glory was just announced. We praise the Lord for sending us such a man of God]

We need to learn that one with God is a majority. Hudson Taylor was called by God to bring the gospel to China. He went with no wife, no denominational backing, no fixed income, and made no appeal for funds. Years later he was asked how he could accomplish such an impossible task. He said:

"It seemed to me that God looked over the whole world to find a man who was weak enough to do His work, and when He found me, He said, "He'll do!" Then he added, "All God's Giants have been weak men who did great things for God because they reckoned on Him being with them."

- **He was asked to do the seeming impossible *Job*.** I cannot imagine going to say North Korea and just start preaching to them the gospel. Nineveh was a huge city and the task given Jonah was enormous. Spurgeon notes:

Is there a servant of God here who feels unequal to his work and therefore wishes he could escape from it? My dear Brother, you are unequal to your work, for you have no sufficiency of your own! I know, also, that I am, in and of myself, unequal to my own calling— shall we, therefore, run away?[37]

- **He was a *Jew* and had no love for Gentiles.** Chuck Smith observes:

"It is interesting that as Jonah was running away from God's call for him to go preach to the Gentiles, he fled to Joppa. He didn't want to preach to the Gentiles and went to Joppa to escape God's call. But eight hundred years later Peter was in Joppa, at the house of Simon the tanner, when God gave him a vision and called him to go preach to the Gentiles (Acts 9 and 10). Jonah ran to Joppa, and Peter was

---

[37] Spurgeon, Charles. The Best of Spurgeon's Sermons from the Book of Jonah (Kindle Locations 32-34). . Kindle Edition.

called from Joppa. God always wanted to reach the Gentiles."[38]

- **He knew they were one day going to *Judge* Israel.** They were sworn enemies, and it was predicted that they would take Israel into captivity. Eventually, a generation after Jonah, Assyria did take the ten northern tribes into captivity in 722 B.C. As Boice noted:

"We can understand Jonah...if we can imagine the word of the Lord coming to a Jew who lived in New York during World War II, telling him to go to Berlin to preach to Nazi Germany, and instead of this, he goes to San Francisco and takes a boat for Hong Kong.."[39]

- **They were pagan Jerks!** Imagine God calling us to go to North Korea, or Iran, or Russia or to ISIS, etc., with the gospel. Nah. 3:1-5

"It's wickedness. A general reference to the city's violence, immorality and idolatry. Assyria was a militaristic society with a reputation for violence and cruelty in warfare. Their religion was polytheistic. Ashur, Adad, Sin, Shamash and Ishtar were the chief deities of the Assyrian pantheon, Ashur being regarded as

---

[38] The Word For Today Bible, Pastor Chuck Smith, p. 1165. Thomas Nelson, Inc., 2005.
[39] An Expositional Commentary, The Minor Prophets, Vol. 1, Hosea-Jonah, by James Montgomery Boice. P. 266. Baker Books, 1983.

the most powerful. The Assyrian gods were patron gods, worshipped for their blessing and protection of specific cities. The patron deity of Nineveh was Isthar, goddess of love and war."[40]

- **It was a long tiring *Journey* to Nineveh.** We are talking about a walk of some 500 miles. John Butler notes:

"No airplanes, trains, cars, busses, or super highways were available for Jonah. He had to go to Nineveh by feet-express, for he had to walk. This would take time, and it would be laborious and even boring...Once Jonah gets to Nineveh the excitement will begin. But he must first make the long walk before he gets there...Some people try to skip the walk...Preachers must spend long hours in prayer and Bible study if they are going to preach well in the Nineveh pulpit...Every duty in life has its walking part."[41]

- **He didn't want to quit his Day *Job*.**

This was definitely an interruption of his comfort zone! He had a nice thing going. A successful prophet with probably a view of retirement in the near future. As one noted:

Jonah had no idea of how self-absorbed he had become until God disturbed his comfortable

---

[40] NIV Faithlife Study Bible, p. 1435, Lexham Press, 2017.
[41] JONAH: The Parochial Prophet, John G. Butler. P. 21-22. LBC Publications, 1994.

life... Jonah enjoyed a comfortable life until God interrupted his dream... People in his hometown of Gath Hepher enjoyed Jonah's preaching and, with his obvious gift as an effective communicator, he soon established a fine reputation as a much loved and deeply respected teacher of God's Word. Early in his ministry, God gave Jonah a prophetic scoop that established his ministry. Jonah announced that the borders of Israel would be extended during the reign of King Jeroboam and when this happened, his reputation was made. He was hailed as God's "servant Jonah ... the prophet from Gath Hepher," as if there wasn't another prophet worthy of the name (from 2 Kings 14: 25)... If he was in ministry today, Jonah would have a full schedule of speaking engagements, his books would be best sellers, and his page on Facebook would be bombarded by fans. Jonah enjoyed a good life doing good work in a good place. He was living his dream until, one day, God interrupted his life.[42]

God has a way of interrupting our lives – an unexpected pregnancy; a death of a loved one; a pink slip from our boss; a hurricane hits; you name it! We don't like change, new things, and the like. What do we cherish most, our comfort or being obedient to God? Jonah's solution was

---

[42] Smith, Colin S.. Jonah: Navigating a God-centered Life (Kindle Location 149). Christian Focus Publications. Kindle Edition.

to quit and head for the hills – or should I say waters.

- **He knew God was *Joined at the hip* with grace, mercy, and compassion.** The phrase "joined at the hip" is slang. It means to be closely connected, always together. Jonah didn't want to go because He knew that God loved to give people a second chance (Jon. 4:2). Is there someone you do not want to see saved? The homosexual, the child molester, the liberals, rocket man in North Korea?

But didn't God give us a second chance, have we not been saved in spite of our past sins, not to mention the one's we committed this very day! J. Vernon McGee once said to his congregation, "If you knew me as well I as I know me, you wouldn't be sitting there listening to me right now!" Then, after a pause, he continued, "But if I knew you as well as you know you, I wouldn't want to preach to you!"

Colin Smith shared these wise words:

Christians are a mass of contradictions. We are righteous in Christ, and yet we sin every day. We have the power of the Spirit, and yet we feel our own weakness... When Christ invaded your life, He opened your mind, changed your heart... The Bible calls this 'regeneration' or the new birth... With this new life, you have a new capacity. God's Spirit lives in you, giving you power and desire to pursue a God-centered life, that otherwise would be beyond both your ability and your interest. All of this is true of you in Christ. If it was the whole truth the Christian life would be easy. But it's not. Your new life of faith is lived out in the body (Gal. 2:20)... The Holy Spirit draws you toward adventurous faith and costly obedience, but the flesh says, "No!" always. Sin inhabits the deep places of the Christian heart (Jam. 1:14)... The source of sin lies closer to home than you or I may want to admit. It's easy to blame God or the devil for our struggles, but the primary source of our sin lies within our own hearts... Sin remains in the hearts of even the most mature believers, and it is never passive.[43]

- **He will look like a *Jive turkey* or a *Joker*.** Remember he was a hero in Israel. He had predicted Israel's boarders would be expanded and they were. If he now predicts that God would destroy Nineveh and it did not happen, word would be out that he was a false prophet. They stoned false prophets (Deut. 18:22a).

---

[43] Smith, Colin S.. Jonah: Navigating a God-centered Life (Kindle Locations 74-75). Christian Focus Publications. Kindle Edition.

Charles Spurgeon, ""Now," said he to himself, "if I have to go through Nineveh and say, 'Yet 40 days and Nineveh shall be overthrown,' and if these people repent, it will not be overthrown! And then they will say, 'Pretty Prophet that Jonah! He is a man that cries, 'Wolf,' when there is no wolf,' and I shall lose my reputation." Do I address any servant of God here who is afraid of losing his reputation?... The highest reputation in the world is to be faithful— faithful to God and your own conscience... Many a man is more a slave to his admirers than he dreams of— the love of approbation is more a bondage than an inner dungeon would be. If you have done the right thing before God and are not afraid of His great judgment seat, fear nothing, but go forward![44]

We are afraid what people might think, so we allow fear to conform us to their expectations.

One of my favorite shows of the past was Candid Camera. It debuted before I was born, on August 10, 1948, Allen Funt used a hidden-camera. It caught people in the act of being themselves. It produced lots of laughs, but it also offered a fascinating look into the human psyche. In one episode titled "Face the Rear," an unsuspecting person boarded an elevator and naturally turned around to face the front of

---

[44] Spurgeon, Charles. The Best of Spurgeon's Sermons from the Book of Jonah (Kindle Locations 49-52). . Kindle Edition.

the elevator. An actor would get in the elevator and face the rear of the elevator. Finally, a fourth actor entered the elevator and faced the rear. Without exception, the person facing the front would turn around and face the rear. The social influence exerted by those facing the rear was too overwhelming for that person to remain the only one facing the front.[45]

Trans: Maybe you have backed down from obeying God because you felt your life would be in Jeopardy; or because it was Just you alone against them; you feel God has given you an impossible Job; not a Jew but just as prejudiced as Jonah against some people; refuse to go to those pagan Jerks; not too happy about God being Joined at the hip with mercy and grace; don't want to obey God because it makes you look like a Jive turkey? I have been guilty of it all, at one time or another, and can only pray God will give me a second chance to change my attitude.

(1). The *City*.

to Nineveh the great city – let's look at a little background material.

According to Ge 10: 11, Nineveh was first built by Nimrod and was traditionally known as the "great city" (see Ge 10: 12 and note). About

---

[45] Mark Batterson, Play the Man (Thomas Nelson, 2017), pages 144-145.

700 BC Sennacherib made it the capital of Assyria, which it remained until its fall in 612.⁴⁶

Nineveh was on the east bank of the Tigris River (near Al Mawsil or Mosul), about 550 miles northeast of Jerusalem (220 miles north of Baghdad). It was not a great city until the reign of Tiglath-Pileser III (745– 727 B.C.). In 701 B.C. Sennacherib (705– 681 B.C.) made it the capital of Assyria and the most powerful city in the ancient Near East, with an urban perimeter of seven and one-half miles. In the same year he attacked Jerusalem. Nineveh fell to the Babylonians and Medes dramatically in 612 B.C.⁴⁷

Located on the eastern side of the Tigris River, Nineveh, the capital city of Assyria, was one of the greatest cities of antiquity. With 1,200 two-hundred-feet high towers and surrounded by a hundred-feet-high wall whose foundation was made of polished stone and of such breadth that three chariots could drive abreast atop it, Nineveh was magnificent to behold. Sixty miles in circumference, enough corn could grow inside the walls to feed the population of 600,000... Hanging gardens filled the city with rich plants and rare animals. Temples, palaces, libraries, and arsenals

---

⁴⁶ Zondervan. NIV Study Bible (Kindle Locations 228294-228296). Zondervan. Kindle Edition.
⁴⁷ Bruckner, James; Bruckner, James. Jonah, Nahum, Habakkuk, Zephaniah (The NIV Application Commentary) (p. 41). Zondervan. Kindle Edition.

abounded to adorn and enrich the city beyond belief.[48]

(2). The *Crying* out against it.

and cry against it, - I like the way the Living Bible puts it:

² "Go to the great city of Nineveh, and give them this announcement from the Lord: 'I am going to destroy you, for your wickedness rises before me; it smells to highest heaven.'"
Jonah 1:2 (TLB)

(3). The Cruelty.

for their wickedness has come up before Me." – This is only the third time in the Bible in which the evil of a people moves God to speak of destroying them. The others are the generation of Noah and the people of Sodom and Gomorrah.

Con:

1. God's command was simple and seemingly impossible – but when we rebel against God our lives become complicated and really impossible extremely fast!

---

[48] Courson, Jon. Jon Courson's Application Commentary: Volume 2, Old Testament (Psalms - Malachi) (Kindle Locations 30586-30589). Thomas Nelson. Kindle Edition.

2. Remember Victoria and Ryan? It could have been like Jonah and the Assyrians, but it ended up more like God and the Assyrians.

3. Nine months after Victoria's ordeal, on August 15, 2005, she was back at her old job. As she walked into the Suffolk County Court building, she watched silently as Ryan Cushing admitted that he had thrown the frozen bird from the car. When the proceeding ended, Victoria waited as the teen walked toward the door. He stopped when he got to her. He began to apologize but broke into sobs before he could get the words out. She took Ryan in her arms and for the next few minutes held him as she stroked his hair. He sobbed and said over and over, "I'm so sorry." She repeated, "It's okay, it's okay, I just want you to make your life the best it can be."

Most of the people in the room were in tears as the scene unfolded before them. The five other teens who had been with Cushing that night all pleaded guilty to lesser charges and were each sentenced to five years' probation. But Ryan had been indicted on much more serious charges, including first-degree assault. He was facing 25 years in prison. But Victoria intervened, secretly meeting with the prosecutor to ask for leniency. At the sentencing hearing Victoria spoke before the court. She said to Ryan Cushing:

"There is no room for vengeance in my life, and I do not believe a long, hard prison term would do you, me, or society any good."

Ryan was sentenced to six months in prison and five years probation. William Keahon, Cushing's lawyer, said:

"I've never seen this in 32 years of practicing law."

Victoria explained her extraordinary act simply: "God gave me a second chance, so I passed it on."[49]

God still wants to pass it on, He could not do it through Jonah, but he could through Victoria...How about you and me?

THE WRONG CHOICE

Intro:

1. CBS News reports that, since its inception in the 1970s, the *Human Intervention Motivation Study* has given second chances to thousands of men and women in danger of losing their families, careers, and even their lives. Eighty percent of HIMS participants never relapse at all, and of the ones who do, most only relapse once. Lyle Prouse, who was able

---

[49] Bathroom Readers' Institute. Uncle John's Bathroom Reader Tales to Inspire (Uncle John's Bathroom Readers) (Kindle Locations 519-521). Portable Press. Kindle Edition.

to retire honorably after a previous arrest, a stint in prison, and entry into the HIMS program, said:

"I've gotten to live out more miracles than anybody I know, I suppose without sounding preachy or evangelistic, the only thing I can attribute it to is God's grace."[50]

2. We have looked at God giving Jonah a Chance at a wonderful opportunity, but unfortunately he makes the wrong Choice. But by God's grace He will be given another chance.

B. The wrong *Choice*. 1:3

1. He fled from God's Plan.

3 But Jonah rose up to flee to Tarshish – As one notes:

Tarshish is uncertain. Its association with ships (1Kg 10: 22) suggests it was near the sea. The "ships of Tarshish" used by King Jehoshaphat on the Red Sea were probably merchant ships of design similar to those used by sailors from Tarshish on the Mediterranean Sea. Tarshish has sometimes been identified with Paul's home of Tarsus in Cilicia or the city of Tharros on the island of Sardinia west of Italy. But the

---

[50] Jelani Greenidge, PreachingToday.com; source: Tony Dokoupil, "Rehab that puts alcoholic pilots back in the cockpit" CBS News (12-10-17).

most probable identification of Tarshish is the Phoenician colony of Tartessus, located on the Guadalquivir River on the southwestern coast of Spain about 2,000 miles west of Palestine. This is about as far in the opposite direction from Nineveh as Jonah could have gone.[51]

Tarshish was in the opposite direction from Nineveh, located in the tip of Spain about 2,000 miles from Joppa. Like the prodigal son he is now headed for the "far country" of carnality.

We must all choose between Nineveh and Tarshish, between God's plan and ours. One of the problems is we tend to live by fleshly impulses instead of the steady Word of God.

Spurgeon has a helpful comment on this:

Jonah felt it come upon him, all of a sudden, not to go to Nineveh, but to Tarshish... It came upon me that I must do so-andso." I am afraid of these impulses— very greatly afraid of them!... Our impulses are not to be depended on... You must never obey an impulse to do wrong! Now, in Jonah's case the impulse was, "Go to Tarshish. Go to Tarshish."... We are no more to follow vain impulses than cunningly-devised fables. The Word of the Lord is to be our leading star in all things... God is not the

---

[51] Staff, Holman Bible . CSB Study Bible (Kindle Locations 191546-191551). Holman Bible Publishers. Kindle Edition.

Author of evil desires and suggestions! It is much more likely that these thoughts come from the devil —and most of all likely that they rise from a foolish and corrupt heart. If anything says to you, "Flee to Tarshish," when God says, "Go to Nineveh," shut your ears against the evil impulse and hasten to do as God bids you.[52]

A December, 2010 article in Newsweek argues that after a brief period of cutting back Americans are starting to spend again— whether they can afford it or not. Some experts call it "frugality fatigue"—in other words, we're weary of cutting back, and we're ready to splurge again. The authors argue, "The truth is that spending may be hard to contain. Entire generations of consumers have grown up with the idea of instant gratification and the credit culture that comes with it."

These are some of the key statistics from the article:

- American households have pared their debt (from $12.5 trillion in 2008 to $11.6 trillion in September of 2010), but most of that came from home foreclosures and defaults on credit cards.
- From the start of the recession, we have continued to increase our spending in the

---

[52] Spurgeon, Charles. The Best of Spurgeons Sermons from the Book of Jonah (Kindle Location 92). Kindle Edition.

following expense categories: Telephone equipment (up 16.6 percent), pet expenses (up 14.4 percent), and child care (up 12.8 percent).
- Although 89 percent of Americans say they're watching their expenditures, spending has increased anyway.

More tellingly, the authors include two stories that epitomize our runaway spending.

Maria Diaz, a 30-year-old waitress who was forced to move in with her mother, said, "I keep waiting for things to get better, and they just don't. After awhile I just decided, 'Screw it. I need some new clothes. I'm going to get them.' My mama's not happy, but I don't care. You stop spending, and you stop living."

Then there's the story of Harry Dugan, a 50-year-old respiratory therapist from New Jersey. Although he's "underwater" on his mortgage and he tried to curtail his expenses, he recently "had a bit of a relapse": he purchased a $900 television and a $21,000 car. "It was an impulse buy," he confessed. "If I could go back, I'd get something cheaper."

The article concludes with a warning: "Yes, spending is great fun, until the bill arrives. That's a lesson we've learned the hard way. Or maybe we haven't."[53]

---

[53] Matt Woodley, managing editor of PreachingToday.com; source:

When we sin by impulse we can be sure we have are going to regret it when the bill comes due.

⁹ Rejoice, young man, during your childhood, and let your heart be pleasant during the days of young manhood. And follow the impulses of your heart and the desires of your eyes. Yet know that God will bring you to judgment for all these things. Ecclesiastes 11:9

2. He fled from God's Presence.

...from the presence of the LORD – there is nothing worse than getting away from the manifested presence of God.

R. T. Kendall writes:

There is an attribute called the omnipresence of God and we learn this as well from the book of Jonah, that God is everywhere...You cannot really run from the presence of God in this sense. You can go from here to Australia and find that God is there, for God is everywhere...While it is true that Jonah could not really run from the presence of God, because God is omnipresent, I want to say this to you: there is nonetheless something precious that Jonah lost. This expression "the presence of the Lord" is used in more than one

---

Stefan Theil, "The Urge to Splurge," Newsweek (12-6-10).

sense…Jonah did lose something. And I want you to know that when you run from God you lose something. It is that special presence of the Lord.[54]

Truth is we can go out of God's presence (Gen. 3:8; 4:16/2 Ki. 13:23/etc.).

It seems bizarre that one would choose to leave the joy of the Lord for the oppression and emptiness of the self-life! Reminded me of a family I read about in Houston Texas. Authorities found an abandoned house in Houston Texas. It said they found, "Recently filled prescription bottles in the bathroom cabinets, books on Marxism on the bookshelves, children's bicycles still leaning against the garage wall."
The people who had lived there was the Lockshin family, they left the freedom and prosperity of America to live in the Soviet Union.[55] What a foolish choice, but choosing our way over God's presence is a trillion times more foolish!

3. He got what seemed like Providential confirmation!

So he went down to Joppa, found a ship which was going to Tarshish, - Joppa, is modern-day Jaffa, a suburb of Tel Aviv on Israel's

---

[54] Jonah An Exposition, R. T. Kendall, pp. 25, 37. Published in the U.K, 1978.
[55] Washington Post, American Scientist Defects to Moscow.

Mediterranean coast. Joppa plays a role in the tribual allotments in Joshua (19:46), where it is mentioned as part of the tribal territory of Dan, and in the post exilic narratives of Chronicles and Ezra, where it functions as the port used to receive the cedars of Lebanon for both the first (2 Chron. 2:15) and the second temple (Ezra 3:7).

If we refuse to live according to the Word of God, we can always twists things to justify our rebellion.

John Butler says it well:

"He found a ship going to Tarshish". That sounds like success for Jonah's plans. In fact, everything seemed to be working out for Jonah in his plan to go to Tarshish. He had traveled to Joppa without incident; and when he got to Joppa, there was a ship going to the very place he wanted to go. How providential! But, as we know from reading the book of Jonah, this was not successful at all...When once a person determines to leave the will of God...the means to pursue it will generally be found – the devil will see to that! There are plenty of ships ready to transport the rebellious person on their evil way...Satan is doing all he can to help and encourage evil. So the person who turns away from God's will and heads out on the road of disobedience is going to find considerable help and apparent success...The Psalmist was observing this when he spoke of "the prosperity of the wicked" (Psa. 73:3).[56]

Spurgeon warns, "Nothing can make it right to do wrong! I pray you, never blaspheme God by laying your sins on the back of His Providence!...Providence or no Providence, the Word of the Lord is to be our guide."... Look at David, too. He is brought out by Abishai upon the field at night. There lies king Saul, sound asleep, and Abishai says to David, "God has delivered your enemy into your hands this day: now therefore let me smite him, I pray you, with the spear even to the earth at once, and I will not smite him the second time!" What a Providence, was it not?... Yet David never said a word as to Providence, but replied, "Destroy him not: for who can stretch forth his hand against the Lord's Anointed and be guiltless?"...Many have erred through looking at circumstances rather than at commands.[57]

See I Sam. 26:7-9.

4. Disobedience always comes with a Price.

paid the fare – disobedience always comes with a price tag.

---

[56] Jonah, The Parochial Prophet, John G. Butler, pp. 34-35. Published by LBC Publications, 1994.
[57] Spurgeon, Charles. The Best of Spurgeons Sermons from the Book of Jonah (Kindle Locations 201-202). Kindle Edition.

Disobedience cost, I use, *MR. PALMER* to remind me of the cost of sin:

- M = Misery. A believer can sin but cannot not enjoy it (Psa. 32:3; 38:4; 51:8, 12/2 Pet. 2:7-8).

- R = Responsibility to glorify God. Sin dishonors God, and the goal of our life is to glorify God (1 Cor. 10:31/Rev. 4:11).

- P = It means a loss of Power (Judges 16:20), of the manifested presence of God (Hos. 5:6), of answered Prayer (Psa. 66:18/Isa. 59:2/Jam. 4:3), and Purity (Isa. 5:18/Prov. 5:22), sin always enslaves.

- A = Agape. It is a sin against God's love (Rev. 2:4).

- L = Loyalty to Satan and Self is what sin really is! We are the Bride of Christ, to sin is to be unfaithful to that union (1 Cor. 6:17).

- M = Ministry is always effected by our persistent sin. And yet we have to be careful here because one can exercise their gift even in the flesh (1 Cor. 13:1-3). Jonah was clearly out of God's will but God still used him to save those sailors.

- E = Eternity. Sin means a loss of rewards (1 Cor. 9:24-27).

- R = Reality is that God's way is always best.

Russ Reaves give us insight:

In verse 3, we read that Jonah went down to Joppa and found a ship that was going to Tarshish, and he paid the fare. You better believe he paid the fare! There are no free rides. We must remember that in the ancient world, as in many parts of the world today, money is something of a sophisticated innovation. I've visited villages in Africa where no one had any money, and no one needed money. If they had money, there was nothing around to spend it on. In the world in which Jonah lived, the economy operated largely without an exchange of currency. And a journey of this distance would have been costly. It likely cost more than Jonah could afford to pay. Some have speculated that Jonah may have had to sell his home and possessions to afford the price of this journey... There was only one problem with his plan. God knew something Jonah didn't know. He always does. God knew that Jonah wouldn't make it to Tarshish. Somewhere in the depths of the Mediterranean Sea, Jonah will be thrown overboard, and there will be no refund on the cost of his ticket. He will be back where he started from, with nothing to his name but a tragic story to tell.[58]

We like to watch Cash Cab, it is a TV game show. I have seen people get $3,000 dollars and lose it all by going for the double bonus video question. Ben Bailey the host usually says, "At least you have a good story to tell." I think, Ben if I just lost $3,000 that is not what I call a good story to tell! When we willfully sin against God's plan we never leave with a good story to tell.

5. Our plan is always downward Progression.

and went down into it to go with them to Tarshish from the presence of the LORD – disobedience never causes us to go up but down. Jonah went down to Joppa, down into the ship, down into the deep, down into the fishes belly.

This reminded me of when I was in Austria at a Navigators retreat and we went skiing. I am not very coordinated and they were trying to teach us how to stop, which requires strong ankles. The instructor knew me by name! As he was talking to us, I would begin to go down the hill, and could not stop! I keep going down, further and faster until I crashed! That is the

---

[58] Reaves, Russ. Jonah: An Expository Commentary (Kindle Locations 1018-1021). Kindle Edition.

way sin is, it always take us downward, farther and farther from God until we crash.

O. S. Hawkins notes:

Once we step on the pathway of disobedience, the road keeps spiraling downward. David started going down when he watched Bathseba bathing. He went down farther when he called for her. He went down farther into adultery. He went down farther when he had her husband Uriah killed. He went down farther when he tried to cover over his sin...This is the way it is in leaving the will of God...If we could only learn this simple lesson: No one ever goes up while in rebellion against God. A lot of people today are fooling themselves. A fall is just what it says it is. People never fall up; they fall down. There is no standing still on the way to Tarshish.[59]

I visited the Grand Canyon when I was a kid. When you stand atop the South Rim, the temperature may be a comfortable 75 degrees, and the journey below looks adventurous. But if you start down, every step farther down the temperature goes up. By the time you reach the floor of the canyon, it's 105 degrees. You are dehydrated and fatigued, tired and have a 6 mile trek ahead of you to get back where you started. Every year, many people are pulled

---

[59] Meeting the God of the Second Chance, Jonah, O. S. Hawkins, pp. 31-32. Loizeaux Brothers, Neptune, New Jersey, 1990.

out of the canyon by rescuers, and some do not make it at all! That is the way the path of disobedience takes us.

Con:

1. Jonah was given a wonderful Chance to serve the Lord but made the wrong Choice.

2. But I want to keep before us the theme of this book, that God will still give Jonah a Second Chance.

3. SpaceX, the California space technology company that has pioneered the science of safely returning used rocket boosters to earth in recent years, recently uploaded a YouTube video showing some of the most dramatic times that it did *not* succeed.

The two minute video, titled "How Not to Land an Orbital Rocket Booster," is set to the song "The Liberty Bell" by John Philip Sousa and includes humorous captions for each clip of impressive rocket explosions.
In one segment that shows SpaceX CEO Elon Musk observing a smoldering rocket, the caption reads "It's just a scratch."
Another chimes in, "Well, technically, it did land … just not in one piece."
The video even pokes fun at the phrase "rapid unscheduled disassembly," a phrase Musk has made famous to describe untimely and expensive explosions of impressive size.

The video ends, however, with triumphant footage of its first two successful landings, one on land and one on sea. The company's success rate continues to rise, and it has successfully landed 16 additional rocket boosters to earth (apparently making it acceptable for the company to publish the footage).[60]

Like Jonah we all fail many times, but it is encouraging to know in the end we will enter eternity successfully.

THE CHASE IS ON!

Intro:

1. Ann and I like to watch shows that challenge the mind, like Cash Cab and The Chase. *The Chase* is a quiz show hosted by Brooke Burns, and features Mark Labbett (nicknamed "The Beast") as the "chaser". He chases people in order to crush their hopes of going home with some money.[61]

At 6 ft. 6 in. 380 lbs. and with a nasty disposition, the Beast is intimidating.

---

[60] Ethan Adams, PreachingToday.com; source: Marcia Dunn, "SpaceX bloopers video: 'How NOT to land an orbital rocket,'" Yahoo! News (9-14-17).
[61] wikipedia.org/wiki/The_Chase_(U.S._game_show).

2. What a contrast with God, when we rebel against Him, He also says, "The Chase is on!" But not to blast us but to bless us. The good news is that God pursues Jonah. He does not let him go and start looking for another prophet who will obey Him, or God could have let the rebellious prophet drown, but instead He goes after Jonah, in order to rescue him, and give him another chance. God never gave up on Jonah, and He will never give up on us (Heb. 13:5-6).

One of my favorite books in the Old Testament is the book of Hosea. God told Hosea to marry a prostitute. He did, loved her and cared for her, but then, one day she just left him. God told him to go get her, bring her back and he found her on the slave block. He had to buy her, taker her back and love her as if she had never deserted him. God says that is the kind of love God has for His people.

I told my wife, if she ever leaves me, I am going with her! I learned that from my heavenly Father.

Trans: We have seen Jonah's Chance, his wrong Choice, and now the Chase. Jonah 1:4. God's Word is clear, His love is unconditional, eternal, and the basis of our confidence. Jonah fled but Jehovah followed! He always does!

See Isa. 49:15-16/Jer. 31:3/John 13:1/Rom. 8:39/Eph. 3:17-18/1 Jn. 4:18.

C. The Chase is on. 1:4-16

1. The Lord's Storm. 4

a. God's Sovereignty.

⁴ The LORD hurled – this is a strong word, in the modern Hebrew the word is used for a missile!

The root twl (" hurl, send, throw") is first used in this verse and three additional times in chapter 1, increasing the sense of power and danger in the situation: 1: 4: Yahweh sent a great wind on the sea. 1: 5: [The sailors] threw the cargo into the sea. 1: 12: "Throw me into the sea," he replied. 1: 15: [The sailors] threw him overboard.

Colin Smith notes, "Literally, Jonah tells us, God 'hurled' this wind, as if He had thrown it out from heaven with His own hand. You could hardly have a clearer or more dramatic picture of God's direct intervention. Storms don't happen by chance. God sustains all things by His powerful word (Heb. 1: 3). The wind and the waves obey Him (Mark 4: 41). That means that storms, floods, landslides, volcanoes and earthquakes happen by God's decree.[62]

---

[62] Smith, Colin S.. Jonah: Navigating a God-centered Life (Kindle Location 348). Christian Focus Publications. Kindle Edition.

God's sovereignty is seen in nature.

- God controls the Weather.

See, Job 37: 3, 6, 10-13/ Psalm 147: 8,16-18; 148:8/ Jeremiah 10: 13/ Amos 4: 7/Mt. 8:27.

I was reminded of something I read, a dense fog halted all flights from the big airport. The lobby soon filled with passengers eager to be on their way. Most of them philosophically accepted the airlines' obvious explanation about the fog. However, one extremely wealthy woman, used to getting her own way refused to be satisfied. Taking a position directly in front of the counter, she rejected all efforts of a young assistant manager to explain the delay. Finally she said, "Young man, I don't believe you know what you are talking about. I insist on speaking to the person responsible for delaying my flight." In a voice loud enough for everyone to hear, the young man said into his telephone, "Hello, operator, would you connect this party with Extension One in Heaven?"[63]

- God controls the Disaster.

See Isa. 45:7/Job 2:10/Eccles. 7:14/Amos 3:6.

---

[63] Bramer, Stephen. The Bible Reader's Joke Book: This book contains a collection of over 2,000 jokes, puns, humorous stories and funny sayings related to the Bible: Arranged from Genesis to Revelation. (p. 162). Unknown. Kindle Edition.

Notice Jonah 3:10, which again attributes calamity to God!

Sadly, we have many Christians, even preachers, who refuse to see God's sovereign hand in disasters because they lack God's wisdom to see how it will fit into God's eternal plan.

On March 1, 1997, a series of tornadoes swept through Arkansas, killing twenty-six people and resulting in hundreds of millions of dollars in damage. To protect disaster victims, the Arkansas legislature passed a bill that would bar insurance companies from canceling the coverage of storm victims, and sent the bill to Governor Mike Huckabee for his signature. To the surprise of the legislators, however, the governor refused to sign it, objecting to one phrase in the bill. The *New York Times* reported:

"Mr. Huckabee said that signing the legislation 'would be violating my own conscience' inasmuch as it described a destructive and deadly force as being 'an act of God.'...He suggested that the phrase 'acts of God' be changed to 'natural disasters.'"

In a letter to the legislators who drafted the bill, Governor Huckabee, a former Baptist minister, explained, "I feel that I have indeed witnessed many 'acts of God,' but I see His actions in the miraculous sparing of life, the sacrifice and selfless spirit in which so many responded to the pain of others."[64]

I am glad the Bible teaches that a personal, wise God, not some blind, impersonal, natural disaster is controlling what happens on this planet.

It's strange even the Insurance companies referred to natural disaster as an act of God.

The key is to cooperate with the Master of the wind! I was born and raised in Grand Rapids, Michigan and it can be very windy due to the size of Lake Michigan. That wind can either help or hinder. If you are walking with it, it can be very helpful but if you are walking against it – you will soon be worn out!

Trans: One of the greatest truths we will ever embrace is the sovereignty of God. Even when we go astray He is working to bring us back to the place where He wants us. Jonah doesn't know it, but he is really not on his way to Tarshish but Nineveh!

In 1876, a small Methodist church near the ocean in Swan Quarter, North Carolina was struck by a hurricane and damaged. It was restored, but another hurricane came and damaged it, and the town, again. The

---

[64] Craig Brian Larson, ed., *750 Engaging Illustrations*, (Grand Rapids, MI: Baker Books, 2008), WORD*search* CROSS e-book, 123.

parishioners restored their place of worship once more, but enough was enough, so they searched for a safer location. They found some land, and offered the owner of the property a generous amount of money for it, but he refused.

Then came another hurricane, and again there was massive flooding, so massive that it lifted the church from its moorings, and sent it meandering downstream. The residents of the town tied ropes to it, hoping to keep it from floating away forever, but the current was too strong.

When the water receded, the building came to rest on that exact piece of ground which the parishioners had previously tried to buy. So they went to the owner and once again made an offer. He refused their money again. He said, "But I'll give it to you, the Lord definitely wants this church on this lot."

The sign in front of the church, from that day forward, said, "The House God Moved."[65]

We may not realize it, but we are moving toward God's will. When Jonah was in that fish, it was dark, but all the while, that fish was moving him toward Joppa!

The children of Israel because of their rebellion were wandering in the wilderness for some 40 years, but God said, "I *led* you through the

---

[65] Dale Fredin, as reported to and written by Barb Lee in The Highland Church Highlighter, Jan-Dec. issue, 2014; submitted by Keith Mannes, Marion, Michigan.

wilderness." And God is leading us regardless of what seems to be. See Prov. 3:5-6

b. God's Severity.

a great wind on the sea and there was a great storm on the sea so that the ship was about to break up. - We can either blame things on some foolish nonsense of man-made climate change or see everything as a blessing from God's sovereign hand (Eph. 1:11/Rom. 8:28-29).

(1) Storms are designed to get our Attention.

See, Psa. 66:10-12; 107:25-28.

Courson notes, "Sometimes God sends storms of severity in order to bring His children into port safely. Such was Jonah's case. This storm was not God's punishment of Jonah, but showed His patience with Jonah. You see, had Jonah listened, through the howling wind of the storm, he could have heard God's voice saying, "I'm not going to let you go, Jonah. I love you too much. So blow, wind, blow."[66]

Truth is God does not punish His children, punishment means to get even. However, He

---

[66] Courson, Jon. Jon Courson's Application Commentary: Volume 2, Old Testament (Psalms - Malachi) (Kindle Locations 30626-30628). Thomas Nelson. Kindle Edition.

does bring about judgment, not to hurt us but help us along the way.

Some years ago I held a revival in North Carolina, on the flight out there I gave little thought to who the pilot was, then we hit a strong wind and the plane bounced. All of a sudden, I became interested in who the pilot might be!

(2) Storms are sent to give us an Attitude adjustment.

We need to realize that no Condemnation does not mean no Chastisement!

Not long ago I had to buy a new outside door for our house. Gary came over and put it in for me. We encountered various difficulties, we had to hammer, pull, and get a little rough with it before it would fit right. Storms are like that, they have a way of getting our attitude right.

Psa. 119:67, 71/Heb. 12:6-8

As one rightly points out:

As believers, if we think we are safe from God's judgment because of the grace that is ours in Christ, remember that the Lord disciplines His own... In the church at Corinth the Lord put His children on sickbeds and deathbeds for profaning the Lord's Supper—

people who had the same grace in Christ that all believers do (1 Cor 11: 30). God can send a storm on one's income; He can hurl a wind on one's health; He can crush one's grades, scholarships, and dreams in school. When we rebel, He can do whatever it takes to get us to return to Him or to take us out of this present life in our disobedience.[67]

Butler notes:

Jonah made the great blunder of trying to get into a "butting" contest with God. No man ever wins such a contest! After the "but from Jonah, there came such a furious "but" from God that it knocked Jonah all the way to the bottom of the Mediterranean Sea! Locking horns with God is a good way to get dehorned...In writing about the Battle of Waterloo, Victor Hugo said it was impossible for Napoleon to win at Waterloo. He said the reason Napoleon could not win was not because of Wellington (the great British general) or Blucher (the great Prussian general) or the rainy weather, but because of God."[68]

When I was a kid we used to play "King of the Hill", being a small skinny kid I was always de-

---

[67] Redmond, Eric; Curtis, William; Fentress, Ken. Exalting Jesus in Jonah, Micah, Nahum, Habakkuk (Christ-Centered Exposition Commentary) (Kindle Locations 358-359). B&H Publishing Group. Kindle Edition.
[68] Jonah the Parochial Prophet, John G Butler, p. 45. Published by LBC Publications 1994.

hilled! But no matter what our size and strength, all will find out sooner or later that God alone is King of the Hill.

You cannot get over the Lord Jesus! He will not let you. Jonah thought he was done with God and his plan for His life, but the problem was that God was not done with Jonah!

The truth is, if you can be completely done with Jesus you never were saved to begin with (Phil. 1:6).

John Jeremiah Sullivan, an award-winning writer had what he called an adolescent "bout with evangelicalism." Sullivan has tried to walked away from the church and a biblical faith, but he can't fully reject the person of Jesus Christ. He writes:

At least once a year since college, I'll be getting to know someone, and it comes out that we have in common a high school "Jesus phase." That always gives us an excellent laugh. Except a phase is supposed to end—or at least give way to other phases—not simply expand into a long preoccupation …. My problem isn't that I dream I'm in hell …. It isn't that I feel psychologically harmed. It isn't that I feel a sucker for having bought it all. It's that I love Jesus Christ …. Why should He vex me? Why is His ghost not friendlier? Why can't I just be a good Enlightenment child and see in

His life a sustaining example of what we can be, as a species?

Sullivan said that "once you've known [Jesus] as God, it's hard to find comfort in Jesus as just another man."

And even after years of trying to live in unbelief, Sullivan admits "one has doubts about one's doubts."[69]

When some were turning their back on the Lord, He turned to the disciples, and then asked, "Will you leave me also." Peter spoke up and said, "Where shall we go, only you have the words of eternal life!" Every true believer is always hemmed into the Lord Jesus.

Why? Because we have a new nature that always wants to follow God; we have the Holy Spirit within, who if we grieve, He will grieve us; there is the Father's woodshed; and the fact that the Lord Jesus is always praying for us.

(3) Storms actually can cause us to Attain to a new level of strength and maturity.

Joseph faced one storm after another but it was actually used to strengthen his faith (Gen. 50:20).

---

[69] John Jeremiah Sullivan, Pulphead (FSG Originals, 2011), pp. 32-33.

A good example of this is certain trees, I read that the more the wind blows on them, the stronger they become, it makes their roots go deeper. The wind makes them more sturdy than ever.

Con:

1. Chase is on!

2. God has a love for us that will not let us go.

3. At age 20, George Matheson (1842-1906) was engaged to be married but began going blind. When he broke the news to his fiancee, she decided she could not go through life with a blind husband. She left him. Before losing his sight he had written two books of theology and some feel that if he had retained his sight he could have been the greatest leader of the church of Scotland in his day.
A special providence was that George's sister offered to care for him. With her help, George left the world of academia for pastoral ministry and wound up preaching to 1500 each week– blind.
The day came, however, in 1882, when his sister fell in love and prepared for marriage herself. The evening before the wedding, George's whole family had left to get ready for the next day's celebration. He was alone and facing the prospect of living the rest of his life without the one person who had come through for him. On top of this, he was doubtless

reflecting on his own aborted wedding day twenty years earlier. It is not hard to imagine the fresh waves of grief washing over him that night.
In the darkness of that moment George Matheson wrote this hymn. He remarked afterward that it took him five minutes and that it was the only hymn he ever wrote that required no editing.[70]

O Love that will not let me go
I rest my weary soul in thee
I give thee back the life I owe
That in thine ocean depths its flow
May richer, fuller be
O Light that foll'west all my way
I yield my flick'ring torch to thee
My heart restores its borrowed ray
That in thy sunshine's blaze its day
May brighter, fairer be

O Cross that liftest up my head
I dare not ask to fly from thee
I lay in dust life's glory dead
And from the ground there blossoms red
Life that shall endless be

During a Senate Budget Committee nomination hearing, Sen. Sanders critically questioned Russell Vought, Trump's nominee for deputy director of the White House Office of

---

[70] thegospelcoalition.org/blogs/justin-taylor/o-love-that-will-not-let-me-go.

Management and Budget. At issue was a blog post that Vought wrote in defense of his alma mater, Wheaton College, in which he said that:

"Muslims stand condemned for not believing in Jesus Christ."

Bernie Sanders asked Russell:

"In the piece that I referred to that you wrote for the publication called Resurgent. You wrote, 'Muslims do not simply have a deficient theology. They do not know God because they have rejected Jesus Christ, His Son, and they stand condemned.'
Do you believe that that statement is Islamophobic?"

Vought responded that he did not consider the statement bigoted in nature, noting that he is a Christian and was stating his belief in "the centrality of Jesus Christ for SALVATION. As a Christian, I believe that all individuals are made in the image of God and are worthy of dignity and respect regardless of their religious beliefs," replied Vought.

Sanders replied stating that the blog post was "indefensible, it is hateful and Islamophobic, and an insult to over a billion Muslims throughout the world."

Sanders maintained that he was going to vote against the nominee.[71]

They can call us Islamophobic, hateful, vote against us, and get angry, but the truth stands, and will, throughout time and eternity. There is salvation only through the substitutionary death of the Lord Jesus Christ Jn. 14:6/Ac. 4:12).

Salvation through a Sacrifice.

Trans: Last time we saw the Lord's Storm and now we see the Sailors Stress and Salvation. Jon. 1:5a, 9-10, 15-16

PS: I am going to take things a little out of order, but I will hit every verse before we are done with Jonah.

2. The Sailors Stress. 1:5

a. They Panicked.

5 Then the sailors became afraid – The word for "sailor" here comes from the root meaning "to salt." Flanigan notes:

The word translated "mariners" [sailors] is a derivation of and cognate with MALACH and MELACH meaning "salt", as in Leviticus 2:13 and twenty-six times more in the Old Testament. Mariners were *malachim,* quite

---

[71] "Senator Bernie Sanders Attacks Trump Appointee for Christian Views," BY MICHAEL GRYBOSKI, CHRISTIAN POST REPORTER, Jun 8, 2017.

literally, "salt-men", explaining why, in many parts of the world, veteran sailors are known as "old salts").[72]

Fear is used by God to get peoples' attention. At first they fear the storm, the creation gone wild, if you will, but then it is assumed that one of the gods is angry, and finally it will turn into fearing the LORD, the Creator which is a good thing.

See, Prov. 1:7/Ac. 16:29/Jude 23.

I had a friend named Earl Berkofe who was raised a Catholic. He said they had a loud clock in their house when he was growing up. It terrified him! It reminded him that time was running out, and he knew one day it would tick for the last time and he would end up in hell. God used that to prepare him for the gospel.

The problem today is we have the wrong kind of fear; people are accused of homophobia all the time, I think we ought to talk about normalphobia, the fear of what is normal and right! Sadly we have very little theophobia, the fear of God!

Note: Only God's Spirit can produce a holy fear! The storm was produced by God, not Jonah, not circumstances, but God. Had there

---

[72] What the Bible teaches, Jonah, J. M. Flanigan, p. 509. John Ritchie LTD Christian Publications, 2012.

been no storm there would have been no godly fear! God's Spirit is like the wind, He moves according to His good pleasure! He alone decides to send godly conviction and Revival, all we can do is set our sails.

I read that a preacher, R. T. Kendall, once took Jonathan Edwards's sermon, "Sinners in the hands of an angry God" and read it from the pulpit. The result was some yawned, others politely listened, one man fell asleep. But what is most interesting is that Edwards himself once preached that sermon with no effect at all! You see it takes God's power, and that power is not something we control and manipulate. Two grave mistakes we make is to beat ourselves up over the fact that we cannot make things happen and two, when things do happen to foolishly think we are the source of it!

PS: These sailors had experienced many storms, but none like this one, because this one was specifically from God for a specific purpose.

b. They Prayed.

and every man cried to his god, - these are Phoenician sailors who worshipped many gods and therefore no god at all! "Each man to his own god." This phrasing, in the singular, shows that the sailors did not share a common god, but that each sailor had a different god.

I remember when I was a kid I used to shoot birds with my BB gun. We were not raised in a Christian home. We never went to church, and I do not remember ever seeing a Bible. But one day when we were in school a tornado passed over the school. We were all herded into the hall. I was terrified! I remember praying, "Lord, if you just spare my life, I promise I will never shoot another bird." He did and the next week I was out sending sparrows to their resting place!

Notice none of these gods could help! Elijah on Mt Carmel (1 Ki. 18:27-29).

Pastor/author J.R. Vassar writes about ministering in Myanmar (Burma) and coming upon a broken Buddha:

One day we were prayer walking through a large Buddhist temple, when I witnessed something heartbreaking. A large number of people, very poor and desperate, were bowing down to a large golden Buddha. They were stuffing what seemed to be the last of their money into the treasury box and kneeling in prayer, hoping to secure a blessing from the Buddha. On the other side of the large golden idol, scaffolding had been built. The Buddha had begun to deteriorate, and a group of workers was diligently repairing the broken Buddha. I took in the scene. Broken people were bowing down to a broken Buddha asking the broken Buddha to fix their broken lives while someone else fixed the broken Buddha.

The insanity and despair of it all hit me. We are no different from them. We are broken people looking to other broken people to fix our broken lives. We are glory-deficient people looking to other glory-deficient people to supply us with glory. Looking to other people to provide for us what they lack themselves is a fool's errand. It is futile to look to other glory-hungry people to fully satisfy our glory hunger, and doing so leaves our souls empty.[73]

c. They Performed.

(1) Get rid of stuff.

and they threw the cargo which was in the ship into the sea to lighten it for them. – many people have the idea that if they could just get rid of certain habits it would save them. Stop using profanity, get rid of those bottles of alcohol, and live as moral as possible.

Reformation is not the same as Regeneration.

Richard L. Dunigan shared this:

At their school carnival, our kids won four free goldfish (lucky us!), so out I went Saturday

---

[73] J.R. Vassar, Glory Hunger: God, the Gospel, and Our Quest for Something More (Crossway, 2014), pp. 35-36; submitted by Van Morris, Mt. Washington, Kentucky.

morning to find an aquarium. The first few I priced ranged from $40 to $70. Then I spotted it--right in the aisle: a discarded 10-gallon display tank, complete with gravel and filter--for a MERE five bucks. Sold! Of course, it was nasty dirty, but the savings made the two hours of clean-up a breeze.

Those four new fish looked great in their new home, at least for the first day. But by Sunday one had died. Too bad, but three remained. Monday morning revealed a second casualty, and by Monday night a third goldfish had gone belly up. We called in an expert, a member of our church who has a 30-gallon tank. It didn't take him long to discover the problem: I had washed the tank with soap, an absolute no-no. [http://www.fridaystudy.org/html/ephesians/ephesians4_1_2.htm]

We cannot get rid of the dirt! We are soiled with sin and getting rid of things just feeds our self-righteousness.

(2) Give it all you got.

¹³ *However, the men rowed desperately to return to land but they could not, for the sea was becoming even stormier against them.* – all their efforts could not stop this storm. They thought they could save themselves by something they could do. Man is always trying to do something to save himself (Jn. 6:28-29/Rom. 10:1-8).

Last Sunday morning everything was covered with a sheet of ice, it was 20 degrees and so I attempted to scrape the windows on my truck. I scrapped and scrapped with little progress. Come Monday morning it was still 20 degrees and the ice was still on my truck – then effortlessly and amazingly all of that ice was gone from my truck window! What was the difference? Sunday there was no sun but Monday morning the sun was shining bright!

The difference between saved and lost is the Son! You can work your head off to trying and remove sin from your life, but it is there to stay. Yet, when the Son of God shines upon our hearts through His death, burial, and resurrection the sin is gone – effortlessly on our part and amazingly based on His shed blood.

Russ Reaves notes:

Religious activity is all well and good, unless one thinks that by attending church enough times, saying enough prayers, and doing enough good deeds one has bribed God into overlooking one's sins. Many have tried. Many bad people have tried their hand at being "good enough." But the storm is not stilled. The sea rages on and continues to threaten them with eternal destruction. Try as they may to work hard to earn God's favor, the words of this text become a haunting epitaph for them: they could not.[74]

They are becoming more and more aware that they cannot save themselves. Colin Smith notes:

God has spoken through the prophet, promising deliverance from the storm of judgment to the entire crew through the sacrifice of one man who is willing to lay down his life. But these men think that they can save themselves by their own effort. They believe that they can survive the storm without the sacrifice. The strength of this impulse to refuse the sacrifice is significant. There is a deep-seated pride in the human heart that says, "we can make it through the judgment of God."[75]

This is a poem by William Ernest Henley called Invictus:

Out of the night that covers me,
Black as the Pit from pole to pole,
I thank whatever gods may be For my unconquerable soul...
It matters not how strait the gate,
How charged with punishments the scroll,
I am the master of my fate:
I am the captain of my soul.[76]

---

[74] Reaves, Russ. Jonah: An Expository Commentary (Kindle Locations 1778-1781). . Kindle Edition.
[75] Smith, Colin S.. Jonah: Navigating a God-centered Life (Kindle Locations 430-433). Christian Focus Publications. Kindle Edition.

Years ago, a leading manufacturing company developed a new cake mix that required only water. All tests showed it produced a superior cake that tasted fantastic. But it was not selling. Research showed it was too simple to be believable. Therefore, they added an egg and it began to sell immediately.

The Devil's recipe for salvation always adds an egg! But you cannot be saved by doing – you have to believe it is done by the work of Christ alone (Eph. 2:8-9). Jn. 1:13

3. The Sailors Salvation. 9-10, 14-16

a. The Proclamation by Jonah. 9-10

(1) His Communication of the Savior?

- Who he is - *He said to them, "I am a Hebrew…"* Albert Barnes gives needed background information:

This was the name by which Israel was known to foreigners. It is used in the Old Testament, only when they are spoken of by foreigners, or speak of themselves to foreigners, or when the sacred writers mention them in contrast with foreigners. So Joseph spoke of his land Genesis 40: 15, and the Hebrew midwives Exodus 1:

---

[76] W. E. Henley (1849– 1903). Found at http:// en.wikipedia.org/ wiki/ Invictus.

19, and Moses' sister Exodus 2: 7, and God in His commission to Moses Exodus 3: 18; Exodus 7: 16; Exodus 9: 1 as to Pharaoh, and Moses in fulfilling it Exodus 5: 3. They had the name, as having passed the River Euphrates, "emigrants." The title might serve to remind themselves, that they were "strangers" and "pilgrims," Hebrews 11: 13. whose fathers had left their home at God's command and for God, "passers by, through this world to death, and through death to immortality."[77]

What he claimed - and I fear the LORD God – this seems a little hypocritical. How do you fear a God whom you are in rebellion against? The truth is we all do it! He is not asking them to fear him but God! We think if we fear God then we cannot sin, but in reality it is when we sin we need to fear (reverently trust) God the most!

It is hard to put the words saint and sinner in the same context, but the truth is every believer is both. I don't know if Nelson Mandela was a believer in Christ or not. But I read an interesting article the other day that all honest believers in Jesus Christ can identify with:

"One of the greatest mysteries in life, is the moral complexity that is often found in the

---

[77] Barnes, Albert; Calvin, John; Clarke, Adam; Henry, Matthew; Spurgeon, Charles H.; Wesley, John. The Ultimate Commentary On Jonah: A Collective Wisdom On The Bible (Kindle Locations 885-888). . Kindle Edition.

hearts of great men and women who live truly great lives. No doubt, Nelson Mandela was a great man, but many of the Mandela pieces have turned him into a secular, political saint. But Mandela stated:

"I never was a saint, even on the basis of an earthly definition of a saint as a sinner who keeps trying."

An article in the Los Angeles Times began with the following questions:

"An irritable man who got cross when he couldn't have his favorite brand of mineral water? A fusser who obsessively folded his daily newspapers just so, who got annoyed if things weren't lined up in their precise order? An aloof man who nonetheless flirted with any pretty young woman he met? Could these accounts really tally with one of the world's most beloved men, Nelson Mandela?"

Verne Harris, project leader at the Nelson Mandela Center of Memory, said:

"In the process [of turning him into a secular saint], all the complexities of this human being, all the flaws and elements of his characters and his life which don't fit just get left out."

The article concludes, "This sinner seemed to know he needed forgiveness. He proved it by pushing others to forgive."

Jonah is clearly a saint who not only begins this book as a proven sinner but lapses back into sin at the end of this book:

¹ Jonah was furious. He lost his temper. ² He yelled at GOD, "GOD! I knew it—when I was back home, I knew this was going to happen! That's why I ran off to Tarshish! I knew you were sheer grace and mercy, not easily angered, rich in love, and ready at the drop of a hat to turn your plans of punishment into a program of forgiveness! ³ "So, GOD, if you won't kill them, kill *me*! I'm better off dead!" Jonah 4:1-3 (MSG)

Paul was a saint who feared God yet had to give this testimony toward the end of his life:

¹⁵ It is a trustworthy statement, deserving full acceptance, that Christ Jesus came into the world to save sinners, among whom I **am** foremost *of all.* 1 Timothy 1:15

I like to think that I fear God, and I do trust and worship Him, but I also know my behavior is often just like Jonah's.

- *Who God is – the LORD God of heaven who made the sea and the dry land."*

> He is Perpetual - Tony Evans writes:

This is the name we transliterate as Yahweh, the self-existing God. This name describes God's personal self-sufficient and eternal nature. The eternal God has no past, so He cannot say "I was." He has no future, so cannot say "I will be." God exists in an eternal now. Time is only meaningful to us because we are not independently self-sufficient and eternal.[78]

> He is Personal – the LORD, Yahweh was a personal God who had revealed Himself to Moses at the burning bush. In the GW Names of God Bible it notes:

I Am Who I Am," may convey the sense not only that God is self-existent but that he is always present with his people. Yahweh is not a God who is remote or aloof but One who is always near and who at times intervenes in history on behalf of his people.[79]

> He has no Parallel - God of heaven, this phrase is used 20 times in the Old Testament, 17 of them in Daniel, Ezra, and Nehemiah. This is not a God limited

---

[78] Evans, Tony. Theology You Can Count On: Experiencing What the Bible Says About... God the Father, God the Son, God the Holy Spirit, Angels, Salvation... (Kindle Location 3950). Moody Publishers. Kindle Edition.
[79] GW Names of God Bible (p. 240). Baker Publishing Group. Kindle Edition.

to Israel but One who was the God of heaven and everything under it. Moody Bible Commentary notes:

They desired to know his personal information to learn more about his God. Jonah provided the answers... the God of Israel as no mere local deity but the LORD God of heaven who is the Creator and Lord of all creation (v. 9)."[80]

Complete Biblical Library, "The God of heaven, a term appropriate to the henotheistic crew, which no doubt indicated the chief god of the audience's various pantheons."[81]

> ➢ He is Powerful – indicated by His Name God or Elohim; and His Work, Creator who made the sea and dry land.

Elohim is related to God's power, as Elmer Towns observes:

Elohim focuses on several aspects of power, strength or creativity. The Hebrew word Elohim is from El, the strong One, or the Creator, or alah, to swear or to bind oneself with an oath (implying faithfulness)... He is all-powerful,

---

[80] The Moody Bible Commentary (Kindle Locations 56651-56652). Moody Publishers. Kindle Edition.

[81] The Complete Biblical Library – Daniel-Malachi, (Springfield, IL: World Library Press, Inc., 1996), WORDsearch CROSS e-book, Under: "Chapter 1".

more powerful than any person in the universe. Nothing is equal to Him in power.[82]

Creator, as one Study Bible puts it, "Jonah described God as Creator and Lord, placing Him above the pagan gods that the sailors worshiped. Paul used a similar approach to introduce God to pagans in Athens (Ac 17: 24)."[83]

Who could be more powerful than the One who created everything out of nothing!

Trans: This is what the lost need to know – they need to know God, who is Perpetual in His existence, can be known on a Personal level, has no Parallel, and is Powerful. This is not only what lost people need to hear but believers as well!

When the Bible scholar N.T. (Tom) Wright was asked what he would tell his children on his deathbed he said, "Look at Jesus." Tom Wright explained why:

The [Person] who walks out of [the pages of the Gospels] to meet us is just central and irreplaceable. He is always a surprise. We never have Jesus in our pockets. He is always

---

[82] Towns, Elmer L.. The Ultimate Guide to the Names of God: Three Bestsellers in One Volume (p. 19). Baker Publishing Group. Kindle Edition.
[83] Various, Authors. The Lutheran Study Bible (Kindle Location 233717). Concordia Publishing House. Kindle Edition.

coming at us from different angles ... If you want to know who God is, look at Jesus. If you want to know what it means to be human, look at Jesus. If you want to know what love is, look at Jesus. And go on looking until you're not just a spectator, but part of the drama that has him as the central character.[84]

(2) His Confession of Sin.

10 Then the men became extremely frightened and they said to him, "How could you do this?" For the men knew that he was fleeing from the presence of the LORD, because he had told them. – He had told them that he was responsible for this storm (v. 12).

He had told them he was in rebellion against God. Honesty is the place to begin! Sooner or later we all discover that the basic problem is in our mirror!

In the movie *Phenomenon*, John Travolta plays an ordinary man (George Malley) who is reborn on his 37th birthday when he begins to suffer from the effects of a rare brain tumor, which actually increases his brain activity. As his capacity to understand things that were once beyond his grasp grows, he sets out to tackle an old PROBLEM: stopping the critter that's been eating the vegetables in his garden. His

---

[84] Marlin Whatling, The Marriage of Heaven and Earth (CreateSpace, 2016), page 129.

previous attempts -- building a taller fence, burying the fence deeper into the ground -- both failed.
But as George Malley ponders the situation with an expanded genius, he decides to take a radically different approach to the PROBLEM. Instead of making the fence more difficult to breach, he leaves the gate wide open. Sure enough, a rabbit creeps out of the open gate and then hops away. While he had been trying to keep the rabbit out, the troublesome critter had been hiding in the garden the entire time!

We have mistakenly thought that the problem was out there, but in reality, it can be found within our own hearts!

b. The Perplexity. 10

[10] Then the men became extremely frightened – as we have noted this is a good fear.

As one noted:

They knew that what they had feared was the doing of His Almightiness. They felt how awesome a thing it was to be in His Hands. Such fear is the beginning of conversion, when people turn from dwelling on the distresses which surround them, to God who sent them.[85]

---

[85] Barnes, Albert; Calvin, John; Clarke, Adam; Henry, Matthew; Spurgeon, Charles H.; Wesley, John. The Ultimate Commentary On Jonah: A Collective Wisdom On The Bible (Kindle Locations 928-929). . Kindle Edition.

People today do not know what to fear, they fear terrorists, the stock market going south, losing their health but fail to see the source behind it all – God Himself! Therefore, there is no fear of God (Jer. 2:19/Rom. 3:18).

See, Josh. 4:23-24/Isa. 8:13/Jer. 32:39-40/etc.

c. The Prayer. 14

14 Then they called on the LORD and said, "We earnestly pray, O LORD, do not let us perish on account of this man's life and do not put innocent blood on us; for You, O LORD, have done as You have pleased." - Jonah was innocent in that he had done them no wrong and they had no reason for taking his life. And yet, this rebellious prophet was hardly innocent! That was the difference between Jonah and Jesus – Jonah was tossed into the sea because of his own sin, while the Lord Jesus was nailed to the cross on account of our sins.

Prayer is a good thing! When the lost come under conviction, they begin to get interested in seeking God.

God uses storms to awake people to the need for Him, it was that way right after Sept 11. David Gill, a New York Paramedic shares what it was like just after the September 11th terrorist attack:

> There's a tremendous opportunity to witness. People are crying for the gospel—this is a great opportunity for people to go out and share their faith. People want to know, "Where is God in midst of all this evil?" and I have the opportunity to talk about the fact that God is a good God, and that amidst all of this evil, there is evidence that God exists. A lot of people are very fearful. The City of New York is primed right now for the gospel—our politicians are telling people the way to handle it is to pray and go to church, and our chaplains have free access to go around and minister to people who are working here [at Ground Zero] and outside of here. I had an opportunity to pray with all my coworkers on my shift. I told everyone that if they didn't want to pray, they didn't have to—not one person said "no."[86]

But Sept 11 has come and gone, and it looks like ISIS is on the run, so people are not as interested in seeking God as they once were.

d. The Propitiation. 15a, 16

(1) The need Explained. 12

---

[86] Dan Van Veen, "New York Paramedic—Touching Lives and Souls," Assemblies of God News Service (9-25-01); submitted by Richard Tatum, Wheaton, Illinois.

¹² He said to them, "Pick me up and throw me into the sea. Then the sea will become calm for you, for I know that on account of me this great storm has come upon you." - How did Jonah know this? It seems obvious that the Lord had told Jonah, remember he is a prophet, and they were given direct revelation from God. He is telling them how to be saved.

(2) They Enacted God's Word. 15

¹⁵ So they picked up Jonah, threw him into the sea, - this was according to the Word of the Lord spoken through His prophet.

Spurgeon notes, "Our Savior selected Jonah as one of His peculiar types… Jesus said on at least two separate occasions to those who sought signs from Him, "An evil and adulterous generation seeks after a sign; and a sign will not be given it, except the sign of Jonah. We believe, therefore, that we are not erring if we translate the details of the history of Jonah into spiritual illustrations of man's experience and action with regard to Christ and His Gospel."[87]

One observes:

They hear that they need a substitute to die— in their case, Jonah— so that they don't have to die for their idolatry of self-effort. They trust

---

[87] Charles Haddon Spurgeon, "Labor in Vain." Sermon no. 567, May 1, 1864. http:// www.spurgeongems.org/ vols10-12/ chs567. pdf Accessed June 28, 2011.

the word of the prophet and cry out to the Lord for mercy on their guilt for killing the prophet. They place their faith in the death of the prophet to stop God's wrath, and their faith produces corresponding actions of fear. This is real conversion… Real conversion means that when someone hears that a substitute is needed, he or she cries out to the Lord for salvation by means of God's substitute."[88] Of course Jonah could not save them, but neither could all those animal sacrifices (Read the book of Hebrews). But like the animal sacrifices, God could use Jonah as a type to point to the fulfillment of those things – the Lord Jesus Christ (Jn. 1:29).

Colin Smith noted:

Do you see how beautifully this points to Jesus Christ? The storm of God's judgment is stronger than you are. You do not have the ability to survive this storm by your own effort, no matter how hard you try. The storm of God's judgment will wreck you, unless you are saved by the sacrifice of Someone else… At its heart, the gospel is about God's storm and His sacrifice. Christ was thrown into the storm of God's judgment so that, through His sacrifice, you would be saved.[89]

---

[88] Redmond, Eric; Curtis, William; Fentress, Ken. Exalting Jesus in Jonah, Micah, Nahum, Habakkuk (Christ-Centered Exposition Commentary) (Kindle Locations 580-583). B&H Publishing Group. Kindle Edition.
[89] Smith, Colin S.. Jonah: Navigating a God-centered Life (Kindle

Russ Reaves writes:

Jonah says in verse 12, "Pick me up and throw me into the sea. Then the sea will become calm for you, for I know that on account of me this great storm has come upon you." Jonah is getting what he deserves for his sin. But Jesus is the One who is greater than Jonah. The message of Jesus for the world is, "I have been picked up and thrown beneath the flood of My Father's wrath so that this sea of judgment may become calm for you. It is on account of you that this great storm has come upon Me." The wages of sin is death. But Jesus had no sin of His own to warrant a death such as He died. Rather, He died the death He died as a substitute, a sacrifice offered in our place, bearing not His own sins, but my sins and yours, so that we may be saved.[90]

Kendall notes, "The mariners saw the need of atonement – outside themselves. We are told that the men feared the Lord exceedingly and offered a sacrifice unto Yahweh…And so it is, you will never be saved until you see the need for atonement and that it must come outside yourself. You need a substitute: One who did what you cannot. And this is what Jesus Christ did on the cross. He did what you cannot do: He atoned for sin."[91]

Locations 442-443). Christian Focus Publications. Kindle Edition.
[90] Reaves, Russ. Jonah: An Expository Commentary (Kindle Locations 1808-1813). . Kindle Edition.

This is ALWAYS the need, the substitionary death of the Lord Jesus Christ. Without His sacrifice there is no salvation!

Why do people reject the need for His substituionary death? They do not really believe that they are sinners!

In his book *Being the Body*, Charles Colson writes about meeting a businessman whom he calls Mr. Abercrombie. He had invited Colson to speak at a Bible study he hosted. Nineteen other movers and shakers of the business world were in attendance. Colson writes about what transpired:

Mr. Abercrombie had asked me to speak at the luncheon and then allow time for questions. Somewhere in my talk I referred to our sinful nature. Actually, "total depravity" was the phrase I used. I noticed at the time that a few individuals shifted uncomfortably in their leather chairs, and, sure enough, it must have hit the mark. Because after I finished, the first question was on sin.

An older gentle man said, "You don't really believe we are sinners, do you? I mean, you're too sophisticated to be one of those hellfire-and-brimstone fellows, intelligent people don't go for that back-country preacher stuff."

---

[91] Jonah An Exposition, R. T. Kendall, p. 74. Paternoster Press.

Colson replied, "Yes, sir, I believe we are desperately sinful. What's inside of each of us is really pretty ugly. In fact we deserve hell and would get it, but for the sacrifice of Christ for our sins."

Mr. Abercrombie himself looked distressed by now. And added:

"Well, I don't know about that, I'm a good person and have been all my life. I go to church, and I get exhausted spending all my time doing good works."
The room seemed particularly quiet, and twenty pairs of eyes were trained on me. Colson continued:

"If you believe that, Mr. Abercrombie—and I hate to say this, for you certainly won't invite me back—you are, for all of your good works, further away from the kingdom than the people I work with in prison who are aware of their own sins. In fact, gentlemen, if you think about it, we are all really more like Adolf Hitler than like Jesus Christ."[92]

We are sinners and without placing our faith in the sacrificial death of Jesus Christ we will end up in the same hell as Hitler did – and for the same reason, unbelief!

---

[92] Charles Colson and Ellen Vaughn, Being the Body (Nelson, 2003), pp. 190-191; submitted by Lee Eclov, Vernon Hills, Illinois.

(3) It worked out as Expected. 15b

and the sea stopped its raging – this found salvation through the sacrifice! This must have confirmed their faith in the reality of the LORD and His power. For the storm to stop immediately as Jonah hit the water must have been an awesome moment.
"The narrator leaves no doubt about who is in control in this story. God commands Jonah, and God controls nature to make sure Jonah does not escape. God's power is used with a purpose, to force Jonah to do as commanded...God's mighty works of controlling the storm's beginning and ending lead to the *de facto* conversion of the sailors. These sailors exhibit fear of YHWH (Jonah 1:10,16) not because God sends the storm but because God controls nature and because God delivers them. Their fear is grounded in respect, awe, and gratitude."[93]

Trans: Substitutionary death of Christ works – all their praying, rowing, throwing, and figuring could not stop the storm. Nor could it improve upon God's simple solution of a substitute.

Zoe Kleinman with the BBC writes:

---

[93] Smyth & Helwys Bible Commentary, The book of the Twelve Hosea-Jonah, James D. Nogalski. P. 421. Smyth & Helwys Publishing, Inc. 2011.

An "intelligent" toilet that opens when you approach it and self-cleans with every flush is on display at the Consumer Electronics Show in Las Vegas. Despite a $9,800 price tag, more than 40 million earlier versions of the Neorest toilets have been sold. Bathroom firm Toto said the new prototype was still in development. Its self-cleaning process uses a combination of a disinfectant and a glaze - made out of zirconium and titanium dioxide - which coats the bowl. A spokeswoman Lenora Compos explains"

"Once it flushes it sprays the interior of the bowl with electrolysed water, the "proprietary process" essentially turns the water into a weak bleach. This bleaches the interior, killing anything in the bowl, meanwhile an ultraviolet light in the lid charges the surface.
That makes it super-hydrophilic - or water-loving, so nothing can stick to it - and also photocatalytic, enabling oxygen ions to break down bacteria and viruses." She said, "You don't have to clean the toilet bowl for over a year."[94]

It is amazing now many new and improved things we read about these days. Even toilets! But there is no such thing as a new and improved sacrifice for sin. There is only one

---

[94] "The toilet you only clean once a year," By Zoe Kleinman, BBC News, January 8, 2016.

way to stop the just, raging wrath of God – the subsitutionary death of the Lord Jesus.

As one so put it, "Electrolysed water can't compare to the waters of His baptism. Ultraviolet light can't match the purifying brilliance of His glory. Oxygen ions and titanium dioxide can't cleanse us from the contaminates of sin like the blood of Jesus. He is the only Savior who can take our sins away, not once a year, but once and for all time." (4) Salvation brings about an Expressed change. 16

- They Feared - *Then the men feared the LORD greatly.* Notice the progression: They feared (1:5); they feared with a great fear (1:10); and they feared the LORD with a great fear (1:16). What I like about his is that they feared *after* the storm. I have known many people who promise God the world while the storm is raging but as soon as the danger is over it is back to business as usual! That also had to acknowledge that the Lord "had done as He pleased" (v. 14b). Hawkins observes:

"A lot of us promise God all sorts of things when the storm is raging and then we forget them when the storm passes by. These men made their promises, and thanksgiving after the storm…They were not saved because they offered sacrifices; they offered sacrifices because they were saved. Works are not for salvation. These men offered their sacrifices after the sea had calmed...They surrendered to the sovereignty of the Lord God. God is sovereign, which simply means He does what He pleases (and He is always pleased with what He does). This is one reason folks do not come to Christ...They would rather do as they please than allow God to do as He pleases in their lives...When we see the reason for our storms and react properly to them, we will see similar results. The raging sea will grow calm. We will acknowledge that the Lord can do as He pleases in our lives, and we will make our lives a living sacrifice to His glory.[95]

- They Sacrificed - *and they offered a sacrifice to the LORD.*

- *They Vowed - and made vows.* – was this a vow to turn from idols and follow the LORD?

NET note is helpful here:

Heb "they sacrificed sacrifices." The root זבח (zbkh, "sacrifice") is repeated in the verb and accusative noun, forming an emphatic effected accusative construction in which the verbal action produces the object (see IBHS 166-67 § 10.2.1f). Their act of sacrificing would produce

---

[95] Meeting the God of the Second Chance Jonah, O. S. Hawkins, p. 57, Loizeaux Brothers Neptune, New Jersey.

the sacrifices. It is likely that the two sets of effected accusative constructions here (" they vowed vows and sacrificed sacrifices") form a hendiadys; the two phrases connote one idea: "they earnestly vowed to sacrifice lavishly." It is unlikely that they offered animal sacrifices at this exact moment on the boat – they had already thrown their cargo overboard, presumably leaving no animals to sacrifice. Instead, they probably vowed that they would sacrifice to the LORD when – and if – they reached dry ground.[96]

The point is Salvation transforms us, and we are never the same (1 Jn. 3:9). It gives us a new regenerated heart, which begins within and works its way eventually outward.

Religion doesn't bring an inner change, but is only a surface work that leaves the inner person untouched and therefore does not work. It reminds me of one of my favorite commercials, by one credit card company, *Capital One*. A couple is making a purchase in a shopping center. When the clerk tells how much it will cost, the woman says she will pay the bill with her credit card. Suddenly hordes of barbarians begin surging into the store. They run down the store aisles yelling, with weapons drawn, toward the couple making the credit card purchase. The point of

---

[96] Biblical Studies Press. NET Bible First Edition (with notes) (Kindle Location 162816). Biblical Studies Press. Kindle Edition.

the ad is that making yourself liable to the finance charges on credit cards is like bringing on the barbarians.

One quick scene in the ad gives us a picture of religion, as the barbarians charge past one store clerk at the perfume counter, she sprays perfume on them!

Trying to civilize a horde of bloodthirsty barbarians, to get rid of their foul aroma, with a few squirts of perfume, is what religion is, it is merely external, it cannot deal with our barbarian heart.[97]

Con:

1. Salvation is only by way of Sacrifice – by the substitutionary death of the Lord Jesus. And that sacrifice was not easy, we will never be able to fully understand how it felt to die in our place.

2. The words of Psa. 22:1 come to mind:

[1] My God, my God, why have You forsaken me? Far from my deliverance are the words of my groaning. [2] O my God, I cry by day, but You do not answer; And by night, but I have no rest. Psalm 22:1-2

---

[97] Craig Brian Larson, Arlington Heights, Illinois.

3. Theologian James R. Edwards retells the following true story to illustrate our need and Christ's response to our need. In August 1957 four climbers—two Italians and two Germans—were climbing the 6,000 foot near-vertical North Face in the Swiss Alps. The two German climbers disappeared and were never heard from again. The two Italian climbers, exhausted and dying, were stuck on two narrow ledges a thousand feet below the summit. The Swiss Alpine Club forbade rescue attempts in this area (it was just too dangerous), but a small group of Swiss climbers decided to launch a private rescue effort to save the Italians. So they carefully lowered a climber named Alfred Hellepart down the 6,000 foot North Face. They suspended Hellepart on a cable a fraction of an inch thick as they lowered him into the abyss.
Here's how Hellepart described the rescue in his own words:

As I was lowered down the summit ... my comrades on top grew further and further distant, until they disappeared from sight. At this moment I felt an indescribable aloneness. Then for the first time I peered down the abyss of the North Face of the Eiger. The terror of the sight robbed me of breath. ...The brooding blackness of the Face, falling away in almost endless expanse beneath me, made me look with awful longing to the thin cable disappearing about me in the mist. I was a tiny human being dangling in space between heaven and hell. The sole relief from terror was …my mission to save the climber below.

That is the heart of the Gospel story. We were trapped, but in the person and presence of Jesus, God lowered himself into the abyss of our sin and suffering. In Jesus God became "a tiny human being dangling between heaven and hell." He did it to save the people trapped below—you and me. Thus, the gospel is much more radical than just another religion telling us how to be good in our own power. It tells us the story of God's risky, costly, sacrificial rescue effort on our behalf.[98]

As I am writing this, Fox News is reporting on a school. Seventeen were killed and fourteen were wounded by shooter, Nikolas Cruz. A person who witnessed the incident said a football coach named Aaron Feis shielded students as a gunman opened fire.

The Marjory Stoneman Douglas High School football team's Twitter account confirmed Aaron Feis' death early Thursday morning.

"It is with Great sadness that our Football Family has learned about the death of Aaron Feis," he was our Assistant Football Coach and security guard. He selflessly shielded students from the shooter when he was shot. He died a

---

[98] James R. Edwards, Is Jesus the Only Savior (William B. Eerdmans Publishing Company, 2005), pp. 160-161.

hero and he will forever be in our hearts and memories"

The Bible teaches us, that we are all as guilty of sin as Nikolas Cruz, and that our beloved Lord Jesus Christ died in our place shielding us from the wrath of God – if we receive Him as our Savior. The tragedy is most will not identify with Jesus Christ as their Savior because they will not identify with Nikolas Cruz as a sinner.

In 1986, five-year-old Saroo Munshi Khan and his 14-year-old brother were searching the streets for spare change in their home city of Berhanpur, India. Saroo's older brother Guddu wandered beyond the station and Saroo fell asleep waiting for his brother's return. A few hours later, Saroo woke up 932 miles away, in Calcutta, eons away from his home and family. He survived on the streets for weeks, was taken into an orphanage, and was adopted by an Australian family and grew up in Hobart, Tasmania.

Falling asleep can be dangerous, Jonah, like Saroo, had fallen asleep, not only physically but spiritually. He was now a long way from where he was supposed to be.

4. The prophet Slept.

Trans: We have looked at Jonah's Chance, wrong Choice, and now we continue on God's

Chase. We have seen the Lord's Storm, the Sailors Stress and Salvation, and now, Jonah's Sleep. Jonah 1:5b-16 [Note some of this we have already seen]

But Jonah had gone below into the hold of the ship, lain down and fallen sound asleep – it is amazing, a violent storm is raging, lives are in danger, and Jonah is sound asleep!

We are warned about being spiritually asleep (Eph. 5:14-18/Rom. 8:13; 13:11-13).

a. When we are spiritually asleep we are *Unaware* of the *Lord.*

The Lord sent the storm for Jonah's benefit! It was to get his attention but he remains asleep.

When we are spiritually asleep, we become insensitive to the Lord's chastisement. People can go through one storm after another because of sin and never see anything wrong.

I had a member once who smoked one cigarette after another. She was always broke and experienced health problems – yet, she could never connect her sin of harming her body (1 Cor. 6:19-20) with her problems!

We have many Laodicean Christians who cannot see their true condition.

¹⁵ 'I know your deeds, that you are neither cold nor hot; I wish that you were cold or hot. ¹⁶ 'So because you are lukewarm, and neither hot nor cold, I will spit you out of My mouth. ¹⁷ 'Because you say, "I am rich, and have become wealthy, and have need of nothing," and you do not know that you are wretched and miserable and poor and blind and naked, Revelation 3:15-17

C.S. Lewis wrote, *The Screwtape Letters*. In it the profound Englishman had the devil brief his nephew, Wormwood, on the subtleties and techniques of tempting people. The goal, he counsels, is not wickedness but indifference. Satan cautions his nephew to keep the prospect, the patient, comfortable at all costs. If he should become concerned about anything of importance, encourage him to think about his luncheon plans; not to worry, it could induce indigestion. And then this definitive job description:

"I, the devil, will always see to it that there are bad people. Your job, my dear Wormwood, is to provide me with the people who do not care."[99]

b. When we are spiritually asleep, we are *Unconcerned* for the *Lost*.

---

[99] 6,000 Plus Illustrations for Communicating Biblical Truths, (Omaha, Nebraska: Christianity Today, 1997), WORDsearch CROSS e-book, Under: "Indifference".

These sailors were about to perish and Jonah could care less!

Greg Laurie notes:

Jonah, however, tucked away somewhere down below deck, seemed to be peacefully sleeping through the great storm. To me, this is a picture of the church in our world today. The world is afraid, and the church is asleep. The world is asking questions, and the church often doesn't have answers. People are dying in their sins, and the church is out of the action, unaware, and semicomatose.[100]

Charles Spurgeon observes:

Oh if only the vision of hell were sometimes before our eyes— that some few of the sighs of a damned soul were ringing in our ears!... for then, starting up like men that have long been given to a foolish slumber, we would gird up our loins, and using both our hands, we would seek to pluck men from the burning, and deliver them from going down into the pit of hell. Men are dying! Men are perishing! Hell is filling! Satan is triumphing! Poor souls are howling in their agonies, and you sleep? [101]

---

[100] Laurie, Greg. A Fresh Look At the Book of Jonah: The hard to swallow truth about disobedience (Kindle Locations 402-404). Allen David Books/Kerygma Inc. Kindle Edition.
[101] Spurgeon, Charles. The Best of Spurgeon's Sermons from the Book of Jonah (Kindle Locations 357-358). . Kindle Edition.

We should care about the lost! Eph. 6:19-20/Col. 4:3-4.

We are having a bad flu season in America, I have heard some say it's serious how many people have died. I read:

As of February 2, infection rates for the 2017-2018 flu season were still rising, higher than those in any year since 2009, when the swine flu was pandemic, according to the Centers for Disease Control and Prevention.
Even more worrying, the hospitalization rate is the highest that the C.D.C. has ever recorded at this point in the season. It has just surpassed that of the lethal 2014-2015 season, during which 710,000 Americans were hospitalized and 56,000 died.[102]

Everybody is talking about it, and yet, something far more serious then the flu is sin! It affects literally everybody! It is so serious it not only brings physical death, but eternal death as well! We alone have the only cure, the gospel of Jesus Christ, and yet, why are we not sharing the gospel? Many of us have talked about this flu going around but have not said one word about the sin problem or the cure. This should not be!

c. When we are spiritually asleep we are *Unfazed* by our own *Lot*.

---

[102] www.nytimes.com/2018/01/18/health/flu-season-facts.html.

He was in grave danger but did not realize it.

Years ago, one Sunday morning I was in my office getting ready for the worship service. It was about 4 a.m., when I hear a loud crash. I ran outside and saw an old truck, it was turned upside down and a car a few feet away from it. They had had a head-on collision! After calling 911, I went over and by the side of the road there was a lady, she grabbed my hand and keep saying over and over, "I'm sorry, I didn't mean too, I didn't mean to fall asleep!"

Like that head-on that woke up that lady, the storm was designed to wake Jonah up! If the ship goes under, he goes under with it!

We might say, "Well if he dies no big deal because, he will go to glory." Yes, but he will lose God honoring rewards. 2 Jn. 8

One company posted a sign, which read, "It has come to the attention of the management, that workers, dying on the job are failing to fall down. This practice must stop, as it becomes impossible to distinguish between death and the natural movement of the staff. Any employee found dead in the upright position will be dropped from the payroll."

Living a life spiritually asleep causes us to be dropped from the reward-roll!

d. When we are spiritually asleep we are *Unknowing* that we are in *La La Land*.

People who are asleep don't know it!

Years ago I was minister of Outreach at South Side Baptist church, I remember one big old burly man who would often fall asleep during the Sunday morning service! It sounded like a bear snoring, but he did not know it. Everybody else knew it but not him.

I pray that if we are spiritually asleep, that God will use this sermon to wake us up.

e. When we are spiritually asleep we are *Uninvolved* in praying for the *Lost*.

6 So the captain approached him and said, "How is it that you are sleeping? Get up, call on your god. Perhaps your god will be concerned about us so that we will not perish."

Why doesn't the church really pray these days? I think if we are honest most of us do not really think it will make a difference. There is an old story, I do not know if it is true or not, but it does illustrate the point.

A bar was under construction in a town in Texas. A local church started a campaign— with petitions and prayer meetings— to try and stop the bar from being built. Work, however, progressed on the building. With the grand opening just one week away, the bar was hit by lighting and burned to the ground. Incensed by this turn of events, the tavern owner sued the church, claiming that they were responsible for the destruction because of their prayers. The church, however, denied any responsibility and any connection between their prayers and the subsequent fire. When the case went to court, the judge read both the plaintiff's complaint and the defendant's reply. After a few moment's consideration, here is what the judge actually said: "I don't know how I will decide this, but it appears from the paperwork that we have a bar owner who believes in the power of prayer and an entire church congregation that now does not!"[103]

The reality is the only one whose prayers could make an impact on that ship was Jonah's! The lost cannot pray for themselves, unless it is the initial sinners prayer to receive the Lord Jesus Christ as their Savior.

In 1980, Bailey Smith, president of the Southern Baptist Convention, upset people by declaring, "God Almighty does not hear the prayer of a Jew."

Many Baptist objected, Pastor Michael Smith of First Baptist Church of Murfreesboro, Tennessee, said:

---

[103] Laurie, Greg. A Fresh Look At the Book of Jonah: The hard to swallow truth about disobedience (Kindle Location 478). Allen David Books/Kerygma Inc. Kindle Edition.

"His comment amazed and saddened me…He seemed not to realize that Jesus was a first-century Jew, as were all of his earliest followers. Certainly, God heard their prayers. In my opinion, he also misunderstood the relationship between God and all humanity. Whatever else might be said, the Bible teaches that we are made in the image of God. Jesus compared God to a loving parent, who stands ever ready to listen to his children. Such a God hears the prayers of anyone."

But Bailey Smith was right, the only way God can honor anyone's prayers is if they come through Jesus Christ, and since the Jews have rejected Jesus Christ as their Messiah, God cannot honor their prayers! Jn. 14:6 stands regardless of how politically incorrect it is!

Again, if we do not pray for the lost who will? Who can!

f. When we are spiritually asleep the Lord will *Uncover* our carnal *Lives*.

(1) Jonah is Revealed as the problem.

7 Each man said to his mate, "Come, let us cast lots so we may learn on whose account this calamity has struck us." So they cast lots and the lot fell on Jonah.

For the casting of lots, see Jos 7:14-18; 18:10; 1 Sam 10:20-21; Pr 16:33; Ac 1:24-26.). God, who controlled the storm, also controlled the outcome of casting lots.

When we confess our sin, the Lord covers it, but when we seek to cover our sin, He will uncover it!

This reminds me of Crew members of an English ship sailing around Cape Horn in the 1870's. They mutinied against their captain and shot him in the head before throwing him overboard, where his body landed on an ice shelf. Forty years later, off the coast of central Chile, an iceberg was spotted. To keep it from impeding the passage of sailing vessels in the area, a couple of men sailed out to blow it up, only to discover the frozen body of a man encased within. After chipping away the top layer of ice, the body was identified as that of Frank Shaw, a sea captain who had disappeared. Thus, the mutineers, who, for forty years thought they had gotten away with their crime, were hung on the gallows in London. Be sure your sin will find you out (Numbers 32:23).[104]

(2) Jonah is Required to give an account. 8-12

(1) Who are you?

[104] Courson, Jon. Jon Courson's Application Commentary: Volume 2, Old Testament (Psalms - Malachi) (Kindle Locations 30662-30665). Thomas Nelson. Kindle Edition.

8 Then they said to him, "Tell us, now! On whose account has this calamity struck us? What is your occupation? And where do you come from? What is your country? From what people are you?" 9 He said to them, "I am a Hebrew, and I fear the LORD God of heaven who made the sea and the dry land."

(2) Why have you done this? 10

10 Then the men became extremely frightened and they said to him, "How could you do this?" For the men knew that he was fleeing from the presence of the LORD, because he had told them.

What we do affects others!

- Abraham's sin in Egypt almost cost him his wife. (Genesis 12)
- David's disobedience in the unauthorized census lead to the death of 70,000 people. (2 Samuel 24)
- Achan's sin caused the entire nation to experience defeat (Josh. 7:11)
- And Jonah's sin is the cause of this storm.

We have on the wall over there a thermostat, if I go over and turn it up too high, we are all going to start sweating. If I turn it way down, we are all going to freeze! Our sin is like that, what we do has an impact on us all!

(3) What should we do? 11-12

^{11} *So they said to him, "What should we do to you that the sea may become calm for us?"—for the sea was becoming increasingly stormy.* ^{12} *He said to them, "Pick me up and throw me into the sea. Then the sea will become calm for you, for I know that on account of me this great storm has come upon you."* – we looked at this previously. We should tell people the only way to be saved is by the substitutionary death of Jesus Christ, which Jonah's sacrifice is depicting.

Bill O'Reilly's Legends and Lies is most interesting reading, jumping around a bit here is what he writes about Billy the Kid:

No one disagrees that Billy the Kid was one of the most ruthless outlaws to roam the Old West... Pat Garrett became famous for supposedly killing Billy the Kid. But his account has long been disputed. Inconsistencies in his story led to him becoming a controversial figure... There is no argument, though, that Pat Garrett shot and killed a man at Pete Maxwell's ranch on the night of July 14. The man believed to be Billy the Kid was buried by his Mexican friends on the Maxwell Ranch... Almost immediately, souvenir hunters started pulling at the grave site, so within days, his body was moved to the nearby Fort Sumner military cemetery. There are many stories that indicate

that Billy the Kid was not killed but survived. O'Reilly relates one of those stories:
Is it possible that Billy the Kid actually survived that night? According to one version, he was badly wounded, but the Mexican women of the hacienda saved his life, then substituted the body of a man who had died naturally that night; Bonney then lived the rest of his life peacefully under the name John Miller.[105]

That is likely fiction, but it does illustrate an actual fact about those of us who have trusted Christ as Savior. We, like Billy the Kid, are born sinners and have grievously sinner all of our lives. But then the Lord Jesus died in our place, as our substitute and rose from the grave and now we have peace with God under the name of "in Christ!"

Con:

1. Jonah was not only physically asleep but spiritually asleep, and thus, a long way from where he was supposed to be, but God is in the process of bringing him back.
2. Remember we started out with Saroo? Well as Paul Harvey would say, here is the rest of the story.

3. Twenty-six years later, he found his way back to his hometown with the help of Google

---

[105] Fisher, David; O'Reilly, Bill. Bill O'Reilly's Legends and Lies: The Real West (Kindle Location 3248). Henry Holt and Co.. Kindle Edition.

Earth. An article explained Saroo's journey back home:

In 2011, using vague memories and Google Earth imagery, Saroo identified his home town. Using the ruler feature in Google Earth, he mapped out a search radius by making an educated guess about how far he traveled by train. After countless hours of scouring this area of Google Earth imagery, he came upon a proverbial needle in a haystack. Saroo spotted one vague landmark that led him to the next, helping him unlock a five-year-old child's memories. He eventually spotted a neighborhood, street, and tin roof that looked familiar.

In Saroo's words, "It was just like being Superman. You are able to go over and take a photo mentally and ask, 'Does this match?' And when you say, 'No,' you keep on going and going and going."

In 2012, Saroo embarked on a trip from Australia back to India. Once he arrived, he shared his story with locals, who helped him find his way back home to his mother and surviving brother and sister. Twenty-six years after accidentally leaving home, he finally found his way back.[106]

---

[106] Emil Protalenski, "After falling asleep on a train as a boy, Indian man finds his way home 26 years later with Google Earth," TNW blog (10-15-13).

Jonah leaving the place where God wanted him was not by accident but pure rebellion, and yet, God is going to bring the prophet back to where he belongs – and our Lord is doing the same for us, destination New Jerusalem!

Chapter Two

SECOND CHANCE RECEIVED

Jonah 1:17-3:10

Intro:

1. I once saw a car, it looked a little like my truck, it's paint was peeling off, it had a gash on the side of it, a window was missing with a piece of cardboard flapping in the wind, and a piece of wire keeping the door from opening. But what got my attention was the bumper sticker on it. It said in big letters: This is NOT an Abandoned car!

2. Jonah is beginning to look like that car – a little beat up, bruised, and bleeding. But he is not an abandoned prophet!

3. The Second Chance Received.
Trans: We have seen that the Second Chance was Required because of Jonah's rebellion, now we see that it was Received because of God's grace. 1:17-3:10

II. SECOND CHANCE RECEIVED. 1:17-3:10

A. First, we have the *Conveyance*. 1:17

1. Jehovah's *deliverance* of Jonah. 17a

¹⁷ And the LORD appointed a great fish to swallow Jonah – not exactly a room in the Hilton, but it did beat drowning.

Chuck Swindoll has a way with words:

"Pitch black. Splashing gastric juices all over you, burning skin, eyes, throat, and nostrils. Oxygen is scarce and each frantic gulp of air is saturated with salt water. The rancid smell of digested food causes you to throw up repeatedly until you have only dry heaves left. Everything you touch has the slimy feel of the mucous membranes that line the stomach. You feel claustrophobic. With every turn and dive of the great fish, you slip and slide in the cesspool of digestive fluid. There are no footholds. No blankets to keep you warm from the cold, clammy depths of the sea."
Such was Jonah's deliverance, I am sure he would have preferred a life preserver thrown from a passing yacht – but you do the crime you pay the time! Rebellion is never a trip to Disneyland.

God will deliver us, but He does it His way! I was doing a revival in Cominto, AR, the Pastor and I were visiting a Vietnam girl who had come to Christ. She had an amazing testimony, she came to America on a little boat, being without food for days. At that time she was going through a financial storm and Bro. Tom had given her a check to help out – but she refused to cash it. As we talked we discovered that she had received checks from various churches where she gave her testimony, but had thrown them all away. She wanted deliverance but her way.

PS: This is where you get to use all of those Jonah and the whale jokes we have been saving:

- A Children's Church teacher asked her class, "What do we learn from the story of Jonah?" An eight-year-old boy put up his hand. "Travel by air," he said.
- JONAH'S MOTHER: "That's a nice story. Now tell me where you've really been for the last three days."
- Pastor: "Just think of it, Jonah spent three days in the belly of a large fish." Member: "That's nothing, my husband spent longer than that in the belly of an alligator." Pastor: "Well, I declare ... just how long was he in there?" Member: "It's almost four years, now."
- QUESTION: Why could Jonah be swallowed by the big fish in one gulp? ANSWER: Jonah was one of the "minor prophets"!
- After reading the story of Jonah and the whale to her Children's Church class,

Miss Martha decided to give them a little quiz. "What," she asked, "is the moral of this story?" For the answer she called on little Katya. Katya thought for a minute and then replied, "People make whales throw up."[107]

Another PS: This was a supernatural deliverance from God, but it is interesting that there have been cases where people were swallowed by a whale and survived the ordeal. The following account is taken from the *Princeton Theological Review,* Vol. 25, 1927, p. 636:

In February 1891, the whaling ship *Star of the East* was in the vicinity of the Falkland Islands and the lookout sighted a large sperm whale three miles away. Two boats were launched and in a short time one of the harpooners was enabled to spear the fish. The second boat attacked the whale, but was upset by a lash of its tail and the men thrown into the sea, one man being drowned, and another, James Bartley, having disappeared, could not be found. The whale was killed and in a few hours was lying by the ship's side and the crew were busy with axes and spades removing the blubber. They worked all day and part of the night. Next morning, they attached some

---

[107] Bramer, Stephen. The Bible Reader's Joke Book: This book contains a collection of over 2,000 jokes, puns, humorous stories and funny sayings related to the Bible: Arranged from Genesis to Revelation. (p. 182). Unknown. Kindle Edition.

tackle to the stomach which was hoisted on the deck. The sailors were startled by something in it which gave spasmodic signs of life, and inside was found the missing sailor doubled up and unconscious. He was laid on the deck and treated to a bath of sea water which soon revived him.... He remained two weeks a raving lunatic.... At the end of the third week he had entirely recovered from the shock and resumed his duties.

Bartley affirms that he would probably have lived inside his house of flesh until he starved, for he lost his senses through fright and not from lack of air. He remembers the sensation of being thrown out of the boat into the sea.... He was then encompassed by a great darkness and he felt he was slipping along a smooth passage of some sort that seemed to move and carry him forward. The sensation lasted but a short time and then he realized he had more room. He felt about him and his hands came in contact with a yielding, slimy substance that seemed to shrink from his touch. It finally dawned upon him that he had been swallowed by the whale.... He could easily breathe, but the heat was terrible. It was not a scorching, stifling nature, but it seemed to open the pores of his skin and draw out his vitality.... His skin was exposed to the action of the gastric juice... face, neck and hands were bleached to a deadly whiteness and took on the appearance of parchment... (and) never recovered its natural appearance... (though otherwise) his health did not seem affected by his terrible experience.[108]

I agree with one commentary which said, "If the story had said that the Lord sent a shrimp to swallow Jonah, I would believe it. You could argue with me repeatedly that there is no way a shrimp could eat a man or that a man could stay inside of a shrimp for three days. If Scripture had said, "The Lord raised up a shrimp and it swallowed Jonah," it would be true. God is the sovereign Creator. He could create a shrimp way bigger than "jumbo" that could swallow a man whole."[109]

2. Jehovah's *conveyance* of Jonah back to Joppa.

and Jonah was in the stomach of the fish three days and three nights – as I shared before this is a wonderful picture of God accomplishing His will in spite of our ignorance of it. That fish was heading back to Joppa, to Jonah it was just dark and slimy, but all the while God was leading. Often it seems like God is not doing anything in our lives, but He always is.

---

[108] Michael P. Green, ed., "Jonah 1:17," in Illustrations for Biblical Preaching, (Grand Rapids, MI: Baker Book House, 1989), WORDsearch CROSS e-book, 415-416.
[109] Redmond, Eric; Curtis, William; Fentress, Ken. Exalting Jesus in Jonah, Micah, Nahum, Habakkuk (Christ-Centered Exposition Commentary) (Kindle Locations 612-615). B&H Publishing Group. Kindle Edition.

¹³ I had no rest for my spirit, not finding Titus my brother; but taking my leave of them, I went on to Macedonia. ¹⁴ But thanks be to God, who always leads us in triumph in Christ, and manifests through us the sweet aroma of the knowledge of Him in every place.
2 Corinthians 2:13-14

It may be a rough way we take, but we are always heading in the right direction!

Barbra Taylor shared this:

Several summers ago, I spent three days on a barrier island where loggerhead turtles were laying their eggs. One night while the tide was out, I watched a huge female heave herself up the beach to dig her nest and empty herself into it while slow, salt tears ran from her eyes. Afraid of disturbing her, I left before she had finished her work but returned next morning to see if I could find the spot where her eggs lay hidden in the sand. What I found were her tracks, only they led in the wrong direction. Instead of heading back out to sea, she had wandered into the dunes, which were already hot as asphalt in the morning sun.
A little ways inland I found her, exhausted and all but baked, her head and flippers caked with dried sand. After pouring water on her and covering her with sea oats, I fetched a park ranger, who returned with a jeep to rescue her. As I watched in horror, he flipped her over on her back, wrapped tire chains around her

front legs, and hooked the chains to the trailer hitch on his jeep. Then he took off, yanking her body forward so fast that her open mouth filled with sand and then disappeared underneath her as her neck bent so far I feared it would break. The ranger hauled her over the dunes and down onto the beach; I followed the path that the prow of her shell cut in the sand. At ocean's edge, he unhooked her and turned her right side up again. She lay motionless in the surf as the water lapped at her body, washing the sand from her eyes and making her skin shine again. Then a particularly large wave broke over her, and she lifted her head slightly, moving her back legs as she did. As I watched, she revived. Every fresh wave brought her life back to her until one of them made her light enough to find a foothold and push off, back into the water that was her home.[110]

B. Next, we have Jonah's *Compliance.* 2:1-9

1. His *Existence* in the Sea Creature. 2:1

*¹ Then Jonah prayed to the LORD his God **from** the stomach of the fish* – he is praying from the fish's stomach not from the sea. The fish is deliverance from the drowning, not a

---

[110] Barbara Brown Taylor, "Preaching the Terrors," The Art & Craft of Biblical Preaching (Zondervan, 2005).

place of death.

2. His past *Experience* in the Sea. 2:2-6

Notice the past tense.

*² and he said, "I call**ed** out of my distress to the LORD, And He answer**ed** me. I cried for help from the depth of Sheol; You heard my voice. ³ "For You **had** cast me into the deep, Into the heart of the seas, And the current engulfed me. All Your breakers and billows pass**ed** over me. ⁴ "So I said, 'I have been expell**ed** from Your sight. Nevertheless I will look again toward Your holy temple.' ⁵ "Water encompass**ed** me to the point of death. The great deep engulf**ed** me, Weeds were wrapp**ed** around my head. ⁶ "I descend**ed** to the roots of the mountains. The earth with its bars **was** around me forever.*

What we see here is that Jonah "prayed to the Lord his God from inside the fish." Then, immediately Jonah begins to recount what happened to him in the sea before the Lord sent the sea creature to deliver him.

a. The *Problem* – he was drowning. 2

² and he said, "I called out of my distress to the LORD, And He answered me. I cried for help from the depth of Sheol; You heard my voice. ³ "For You had cast me into the deep, Into the heart of the seas, And the current *engulfed me. All Your breakers and billows passed over me. ⁴ "So I said, 'I have been expelled from Your sight. Nevertheless I will look again toward Your holy temple.' ⁵ "Water encompassed me to the point of death. The great deep engulfed me, Weeds were wrapped around my head. ⁶ "I descended to the roots of the mountains. The earth with its bars was around me forever* – this is poetic language, of a literal experience. Colin Smith notes:

When he first hit the water, Jonah worked hard to stay on the surface, but the currents kept pulling him under. Bobbing up and down, fighting for air and for his life, he managed to catch a breath, only to find another wave crashing over him, and taking him under again. With waves pounding him from above and currents pulling him from below, it wasn't long before Jonah went down…God allowed Jonah to go to the bottom before He sent the fish. When, as Jonah says, "To the roots of the mountains I sank down" (v. 6), he clearly was no longer above the water. If Jonah could have stayed at the surface, he might have been able to hold on to some floating cargo and save himself. But God took Jonah down to the bottom, where he had no way out. His strength was gone; he was absolutely helpless. Then God sent the fish.[111]

---

[111] Smith, Colin S.. Jonah: Navigating a God-centered Life (Kindle Locations 515-518). Christian Focus Publications. Kindle Edition.

We can learn several things from Jonah's experience:

- We can learn the value of Mediating on the Psalms. This prayer is full of quotes from the Psalms. The psalms are a great source of encouragement, as is all of the Word of God. Greg Laurie observes:

This is an amazing prayer. What makes it even more remarkable is that the prophet quotes eight times from the book of Psalms, which must have been one of his favorite books. That's why it's so wonderful to memorize Scripture; you never know when you will find yourself in a tight spot and need the comfort and instruction of God's Word. When I pray, I like to quote the Scriptures. It's not to remind God of what He has said, but it's to remind me of what He has said.[112]

Anatoly Shcharansky labored 13 years in a Soviet labor camp. He was released in February 1986 as part of an East-West exchange. Upon leaving the guards tried to take his book of Psalms. He said on Israeli television: "They took all my possessions from me, I said I would not leave the country without the Psalms, which helped me so much. I lay down in the snow and said, 'Not another step.'" [113]

---

[112] Laurie, Greg. A Fresh Look At the Book of Jonah: The hard to swallow truth about disobedience (Kindle Locations 591-594). Allen David Books/Kerygma Inc. Kindle Edition.

- God is the One who is the *Making* of our *Problems*. Notice it shows that the one behind our problems is God, he says, "For YOU cast me into the deep." I thought it was the sailors! Like Joseph, it was his brothers that threw him into the pit and sold him to an Egyptian Caravan, but Joseph knew the one behind it all was God (Gen. 45:5; 50:19-20). We do well to stop talking about bad luck, or blaming people, or the Devil.

- Living in sin, *Makes* us, not want to *Pray*. Up until this time, Jonah never prays. And it is not, that God will not hear us when we sin, but we simply do not want to pray. The truth is when we sin, is when we need Him most! We should learn to keep on praying whether we have sinned or not!

Martin Luther observes, "Some say, "I would feel better about God hearing my prayer if I were more worthy and lived a better life."...Prayer must not be based on or depend on your personal worthiness or the quality of the prayer itself; rather, it must be based on the unchanging truth of God's promise. If the prayer is based on itself or on anything else besides God's promise, then it's a false prayer

---

[113] nytimes.com/1986/02/13/world/schraransky-tells-how-he-clung-to-psalms-captors-tried-to-seize.html.

that deceives you—... We pray because we are unworthy to pray. Our prayers are heard precisely because we believe that we are unworthy. We become worthy to pray when we risk everything on God's faithfulness alone... For your worthiness doesn't help you, and neither does your unworthiness hinder you. A lack of faith is what condemns you, but confidence in God is what makes you worthy."[114]

b. The *Provision* – the fish. 3-6

But You have brought up my life from the pit, O LORD my God. – God did that by way of this fish. I wonder how long he was splashing about before God sent that fish? Russ Reaves notes:

But we are not told how much time elapsed between those two events. When Jonah hits the water, the pace of the narrative in Jonah becomes like a slow motion dramatic scene in a movie. It is safe to assume that it wasn't days, and unlikely hours. We don't know, however, if there were seconds or minutes that elapsed between the time Jonah entered the sea and the time Jonah entered the fish. We do know that it was long enough for him to pray. In the opening words of Chapter 2 we read, "Then Jonah prayed to the Lord his God from the stomach of the fish." This is the first time

---

[114] Luther, Martin; Luther, Martin. Faith Alone: A Daily Devotional (Kindle Locations 426-427). Zondervan. Kindle Edition.

in the whole book that we have seen Jonah in prayer. But it is not the first time he has prayed. In this prayer from inside the belly of the fish, he is recounting how God answered another prayer he prayed while he was drowning in the sea.[115]

c. The *Promise*. 2:7-9

*7 "While I was fainting away, I remembered the LORD, And my prayer came to You, Into Your holy temple. 8 "Those who regard vain idols Forsake their faithfulness, 9 But I **will** sacrifice to You With the voice of thanksgiving. That which I have vowed I **will** pay. Salvation is from the LORD."* – obviously God did not deliver Jonah from the Sea to be digested by this Sea Creature. God did not deliver us from hell to forsake us in this life!

He didn't bring us this far to leave us;
He didn't teach us to swim to let us drown;
He didn't build His home in us to move away;
He didn't lift us up to let us down!

We must not "throw away our confidence, which has a great reward" (Heb. 10:35). As one notes:

A battle rages in his soul while he struggles in the water. Faith rises within him, and he says,

---

[115] Reaves, Russ. Jonah: An Expository Commentary (Kindle Locations 2112-2118). . Kindle Edition.

I'm going to cry out to God; I'm going to put my hope in Him. "Yet I will look again toward your holy temple."... It is a marvelous statement of faith... The flesh will tell you that God is against you, that you have gone too far and that He is no longer interested in you. But faith defies the flesh. It contradicts Satan's lies. It rises up against defeat, gloom and despair and finds hope in God... Faith prevails over despair when you fix your eyes on the grace of God rather than your own failure... When Jonah looked at himself, he despaired because he knew that he deserved to be banished. But then he dared to believe that there is hope in God and that he could find it by looking away from himself and his failures, and fixing his eyes on God and His grace. 'Looking' is a way of describing faith. The analogy goes back to an occasion when God's people were afflicted by venomous snakes during their years in the desert. With people all over the camp writhing in pain from the snakebites, and losing strength by the minute, the Israelites asked Moses to pray. God told Moses to make a bronze snake and put it on a pole. Then He gave this promise: "Anyone who is bitten can look at it [the bronze snake] and live" (Num. 21: 8).[116]

Notice the object of our faith is not ourselves but God Himself – salvation is of the Lord!

---

[116] Smith, Colin S.. Jonah: Navigating a God-centered Life (Kindle Locations 591-593). Christian Focus Publications. Kindle Edition.

Trent Butler notes, "God had saved him. Standing at death's door, he cried for God's help and found God present at death's door. God had truly saved the prophet, and he wanted everyone to know about it."[117]

Question: Did Jonah die in that fish? No!

- *Logical* sequence does not seem to indicate that Jonah died. We have a prepared fish that swallows Jonah, he is then seen as praying inside of the fish, where he is for 3 days and nights until he is spit out onto dry land.

- *Listening* to the text, it does not say that Jonah died.

- *Literalism* is pushing a type too far. Jesus said **"as** Jonah was three days and nights in the belly of the fish so shall the son of man be…" (Mt. 12:39, 41). The argument goes, since Jesus died Jonah must also die. However, Jonah is a type, and they cannot be pushed too far. Isaac is a type of Christ's resurrection, but he did not actually die (Heb. 11:17-19).

- The *Language* of 2:2 is given as proof that Jonah died, but he is quoting from the Psalms, and David often speaks of

---

[117] Butler, Trent. Holman Old Testament Commentary - Hosea, Joel, Amos, Obadiah, Jonah, Micah (p. 288). B&H Publishing Group. Kindle Edition.

being in Sheol, yet he was not actually dead. It simply speaks of a close brush with death (Psa. 18:4-6; 30:3; etc.).

MacArthur is helpful:

The phrase does not necessarily indicate that Jonah actually died. "Sheol" frequently has a hyperbolic meaning in contexts where it denotes a catastrophic condition near death (Ps 30: 3). Later Jonah expressed praise for his deliverance "from the pit" (v. 6), speaking of his escape from certain death.[118]

- The *Linguistics* of a whale or other large fish does not necessitate a death. As one notes:

It is not impossible to survive in a whale. A sulphur-bottom whale and a whale shark have no teeth. They feed by submerging their lower jaw and straining out the water, swallowing any food. In 1933, a one hundred foot sulphur bottom whale was captured off the coast of Cape Cod. The mouth was about twelve feet wide, big enough to swallow a horse. These kinds of whales have four to six compartments in their stomachs. A man could find lodging in any one of these compartments. In the head of this whale is a wonderful air storage chamber. It is an enlargement of the nasal sinus passage

---

[118] MacArthur, John F.. The MacArthur Study Bible, NASB (Kindle Locations 176279-176280). Thomas Nelson. Kindle Edition.

measuring seven feet high, seven feet wide, and fourteen feet long. If the whale has an unwelcome guest, giving him headaches, he swims to land and rids of his offenders.
The *Cleveland Plain Dealer* newspaper quoted an article by Dr. Ransome Harvey who stated that a dog was lost overboard from a ship. It was found six days later in the head of a whale, alive and barking. Frank Bullen, who wrote *"The Cruise of Cathalot"* tells of a fifteen foot shark found in a whale's stomach. He states that when a whale is dying, it empties the contents of its stomach.[119]

Having said all that I personally agree with Tozer who writes:

I receive a lot of magazines, most of which I dutifully and joyously never read. I looked at one recently after I came home in the evening, and it had a question and answer department in it.
One question was: "Dear Doctor So and So: What about the whale swallowing Jonah? Do you believe that?" And the good doctor replied: "Yes, I believe it. Science proves that there are whales big enough to swallow men."
I folded the magazine, and laid it down, for that man had come up to bat, but he had struck out beautifully. For I believe that Jonah was swallowed by a whale, not because a

---

[119] Rod Mattoon, *Mattoon's Treasures – Treasures from Jonah*, (Springfield, IL: Lincoln Land Baptist Church, *n.d.*), WORD*search* CROSS e-book, 60-61.

scientist has crawled in and measured a whale's belly, and come out and said, "Yes, God can do that." If God said that Jonah was swallowed by a whale, then the whale swallowed Jonah, and we do not need a scientist to measure the gullet of the whale....Grant me God and miracles take care of themselves.[120]

C. Jonah's *Second Chance.* 2:10; 3:1

1. God's *Command*.

10 Then the LORD commanded the fish, and it vomited Jonah up onto the dry land. – Jonah is having an Ebenezer Scrooge experience, He is given another chance.

One of the world's worst stinks, under the right conditions, can be turned into the world's most attractive scents. Ken Wilman learned all about this after his dog became overly interested in what looked like a rock lying on a beach. Curious, he picked it up, sniffed it, and dropped it with an 'urgh.
After a bit of research Wilman learned the stinky object is actually whale vomit (called ambergris) and quite rare and highly prized by perfume makers. Under the heat of the sun the pungent ambergris turns from horrifically offensive to the most pleasant of smells. A

---

[120] A. W. Tozer, *The Tozer Topical Reader – Volume Two*, comp. Ron Eggert, (Camp Hill, PA: WingSpread Publishers, 2007), WORD*search* CROSS e-book, Under: "1104. Science; Miracles: belief in".

French dealer has already offered Wilman over $50,000 for his seven pound chunk of whale up-chuck.[121]

That Vomit was Jonah! God's precious prophet! We are not sure where God had the fish spit him out, most think it was Joppa.

Interesting Rabbinic sources take one of two ways of interpreting this, "either by assuming that the oceans were connected underground to a body of water closer to Nineveh, or by claiming that Jonah became a projectile spewed several hundred miles from the ocean to Assyria."[122]

2. God's second *Commission*.

1 Now the word of the LORD came to Jonah the second time, saying, Jonah 3:1

a. The Principle – another chance.

Have you ever played Scribble? Someone draws a wild senseless line on a piece of paper and then you make something meaningful out of it – a building or flower or person, etc.

The wild senseless line is our sin and God's grace makes something meaningful out of it. Rom. 5:20, our sin no matter how grievous or

---

[121] Yahoo News Blog "The Slideshow".
[122] Smyth & Helwys Bible Commentary, The Book of the Twelve Hosea-Jonah, James D. Nogalski, p. 433. Smyth & Helwys Publishing, Inc.

many is always limited, finite; while God's grace is infinite, unlimited. Our sin is no match for God's grace!

The problem is we make more of our sin than God's grace. Grace is God giving the guilty that which they do not deserve.

Charles Stanley notes, "Did Jonah deserve a second chance to carry out God's assignment? No. Neither do we. But God, in His mercy, is not about keeping score but is about shaping us into the likeness of His Son."[123]

Former President George Bush was a Navy Pilot during WW II. During a mission he was hit by Japanese gunfire and had to bail out. It went badly – he slammed his head against part of the airplane cutting and bruising himself badly. It also tore his parachute, causing him to go down faster then he wanted, if he had not landed in the water it might have killed him.

The failure bothered him for years, so on March 25, 1997, at the age of 72 he got another chance to do it right. He jumped from a plane, in the Arizona desert and made a soft landing, 40 yards from the target. He said, "I'm a new man, I go home exhilarated!"

---

[123] Stanley, Charles F.. The Charles F. Stanley Life Principles Bible, NASB (Kindle Locations 66011-66012). Thomas Nelson. Kindle Edition.

Then on his 90th birthday he did it again!

It is wonderful to get a another chance – like Jonah, and many others in the Bible, we have all had that amazing grace experience many, many times.

b. The Pattern.

- Adam – he was clearly warned not to partake of that tree and He willfully rebelled. God could have been done with Adam and just could have made another man! But He gives Adam a second chance.

- Abraham – told to leave his kindred and go to a land that God would show him. He takes his father and Nephew and goes to Haran for about 6 years! But God speaks to him again with the same message.

- Moses –jumps the gun and decides to deliver the children of Israel – one Egyptian at a time. He murders a man, but God comes to him again at the burning bush.

- Judges – the entire book is about failure and another chance.

- David – commits adultery and murder and yet is restored.

- Peter – denies the Lord and yet is key note speaker on Day of Pentecost.

- John Mark – deserts Paul and Barnabas during their first missionary journey, and yet, writes the Gospel of Mark and later is called useful to Paul.

- Question: How many of us received Christ when we first heard the gospel? Did we really deserve another chance to hear it again!

Charles Swindoll noted:

"When God calls individuals into His vineyard, He calls only sinful people. Each inadequate in himself, weak and wayward by nature, and could pose for a portrait painted in the lyrics of the beloved hymn "Prone to wander, Lord I feel it; Prone to leave the God I love." Demas, "having loved this present world" forsook Paul and fled to Thessalonica…Gehazi, Elisha's servant couldn't hide his materialism and greed. Isaiah admitted he was a "man of unclean lips." Aaron prompted the molding of a golden calf for the Hebrews to worship, and Samson was a notorious womanizer…No one is immune to imperfection. None of the above and neither are you nor I."

Again this is not to encourage or excuse sin, remember when we sin we are miserable and lose rewards. I have car insurance but that does not encourage me to run my truck into a tree!

Con:

1. Nothing more wonderful than having a second change!

2. But when you think about it we get something far greater than just another chance. We began by talking about that old, beat up car that had the bumper sticker – This is not an abandoned car. God will not abandon us, but it's even better than that.

3. There is a television show called Overhaulin'. On this show, a crew of expert mechanics set up a fake car theft. The owner is obviously stressed out at the thought of his car being stolen. The crew takes a week and transforms the car to a completely overhauled masterpiece. We're talking about a new paint job, custom body modifications, an all new interior, and a new engine under the hood! When they finally reveal the overhauled car to the owner they can hardly believe it is the same car! The car has been radically transformed. And it did not cost the car owner a dime! It is all completely free.

God not only gives us a second chance, but also will one day give us a glorified body, soul, and spirit! And all by way of the merit of the Lord Jesus Christ. Jonah is not only going to get another chance to go to Nineveh, but will go to glory as well! We, likewise, not only get a second chance but the ultimate eternal chance!

Charles Swindoll gives us a good summary:

"Take Jonah. No one else wanted to…He was prejudiced, stubborn, openly rebellious, and spiritually insensitive. Other prophets ran to the Lord. He ran from Him! Others declared the promises of God with fervent zeal. Not Jonah, he was about as motivated as a 600 lb grizzly in mid January. Somewhere down the line the prophet got his inner directions cross-wired. He wound up, of all places, on a ship in the Mediterranean Sea bound for a place named Tarshish, as you may remember. Through a traumatic chain of events, Jonah began to get his head together in the digestive track of a gigantic fish. For the first time, in a long time, the prophet brushed up on his prayer life. Yelled for mercy, Recited palms. Promised to keep his vow…and so up came the prophet, who hit the road running – toward Nineveh."

He is a marvelous example of how awesome God's grace really is.

3. Jonah's *Communication* of a message. 3:2-10

Trans: We have seen God's Command, God's second Commission, and now Jonah's

Communication to the people of Nineveh. I like the way one person described it:

So you're walking along the beach minding your own business, and all of a sudden this big fish slides himself up on shore, pukes all over, and slides back into the water. Out of the slime and fish parts and seaweed, a man drags himself out, struggles, and stands up — his clothes half digested, a piece of seaweed stuck to the side of his face. He looks at you, coughs up some seawater, clears his throat, and says, "Repent!" What would you do? I know what I'd do: I'd repent!"[124]

a. *Immediate obedience.* 2-3a

2 "Arise, go to Nineveh the great city and proclaim to it the proclamation which I am going to tell you." 3 So Jonah arose and went to Nineveh according to the word of the LORD.
– how refreshing!

Philip is a good example of the need to obey God immediately.

26 But an angel of the Lord spoke to Philip saying, "Get up and go south to the road that descends from Jerusalem to Gaza." (This is a desert road.) 27 So he got up and went; and

---

[124] Bramer, Stephen. The Bible Reader's Joke Book: This book contains a collection of over 2,000 jokes, puns, humorous stories and funny sayings related to the Bible: Arranged from Genesis to Revelation. (p. 184). Unknown. Kindle Edition.

there was an Ethiopian eunuch, a court official of Candace, queen of the Ethiopians, who was in charge of all her treasure; and he had come to Jerusalem to worship, [28] and he was returning and sitting in his chariot, and was reading the prophet Isaiah. [29] Then the Spirit said to Philip, "Go up and join this chariot." [30] Philip ran up and heard him reading Isaiah the prophet, and said, "Do you understand what you are reading?" [31] And he said, "Well, how could I, unless someone guides me?" And he invited Philip to come up and sit with him. [32] Now the passage of Scripture which he was reading was this: "HE WAS LED AS A SHEEP TO SLAUGHTER; AND AS A LAMB BEFORE ITS SHEARER IS SILENT, SO HE DOES NOT OPEN HIS MOUTH. [33] "IN HUMILIATION HIS JUDGMENT WAS TAKEN AWAY; WHO WILL RELATE HIS GENERATION? FOR HIS LIFE IS REMOVED FROM THE EARTH." [34] The eunuch answered Philip and said, "Please *tell me,* of whom does the prophet say this? Of himself or of someone else?" [35] Then Philip opened his mouth, and beginning from this Scripture he preached Jesus to him. [36] As they went along the road they came to some water; and the eunuch said, "Look! Water! What prevents me from being baptized?" [37] [And Philip said, "If you believe with all your heart, you may." And he answered and said, "I believe that Jesus Christ is the Son of God."] [38] And he ordered the chariot to stop; and they both went down into the water, Philip as well as the eunuch, and he baptized him. [39] When they came up out of the water, the Spirit of the Lord snatched Philip away; and the eunuch no longer saw him, but went on his way rejoicing. ^{40} But Philip found himself at Azotus, and as he passed through he kept preaching the gospel to all the cities until he came to Caesarea. Acts 8:26-40 (NASB)

If Philip had waited, he would have missed the opportunity. He had to run as it was to catch the chariot.

It is so easy for us to become distracted from obeying God immediately.

Eighteen year old Fabian Gonzalez was a bright, talented, motivated high school senior on the brink of graduation. Waiting for him in the fall was a $32,000 scholarship to attend Northwood University. But before he could realize his dreams or explore his full potential, his life was cut short in a tragic traffic accident. But unlike so many other teen traffic accidents, there were no drugs, no alcohol, no crazy antics. Fabian didn't die recklessly trying to dodge the rules. He died recklessly trying to obey them. WFAA News, Dallas, reports:

His memory brings smiles to the faces of Ricardo and Priscilla Gonzalez. They recall how Fabian never wanted to upset them.
But on Saturday night, just after midnight, in the 4200 block of South Walton Walker Boulevard, Fabian died trying. Ricardo admits

his son was speeding. "He was in a rush trying to get home, because we gave him a curfew," he said. It's unclear what distracted young Fabian that night last month (April '13) that he should lose track of time and find himself racing to meet his parents' curfew--and expectations. Had Fabian not allowed himself to become distracted, he would likely have left for home in a timely way, driven the speed limit, and arrived alive.[125]

b. The *Immensity* of the *Place*. 3b

Now Nineveh was an exceedingly great city, a three days' walk – some people make a big deal about the fact that the historical city at that time was not that big. They take this to mean that it took Jonah 3 days to walk through the city. Delitzsch is helpful:

This line of argument, the intention of which is to prove the absurdity of the narrative, is based upon the perfectly arbitrary assumption that Jonah went through the entire length of the city in a straight line, which is neither probable in itself, nor implied... This simply means to enter, or go into the city, and says nothing about the direction of the course he took within the city. But in a city, the diameter of which was 150 stadia, and the circumference 480 stadia, one might easily

---

[125] "Dallas teen died speeding to meet parental curfew" by Shon Gables, WFAA News, Dallas, 4/7/13.

walk for a whole day without reaching the other end, by winding about from one street into another. And Jonah would have to do this to find a suitable place for his preaching, since we are not warranted in assuming that it lay exactly in the geographical centre, or at the end of the street which led from the gate into the city. But if Jonah wandered about in different directions, as Theodoret says, "not going straight through the city, but strolling through market-places, streets, etc.," the distance of a day's journey over which he travelled must not be understood as relating to the diameter or length of the city; so that the objection to the general opinion, that the three days' journey given as the size of the city refers to the circumference, entirely falls to the ground.[126]

c. The *Imminent Menace*. 4

(1) The *Depravity*.

² *"Arise, go to Nineveh the great city and cry against it, for their wickedness has come up before Me."* – we already looked at this but need to be reminded that God's judgment was just.

Today we have all but eliminated the concept of evil and wickedness. We have all of these

---

[126] C. F. Keil, *Commentary on the Old Testament – Volume 10: The Minor Prophets*, (Edinburgh: T. & T. Clark, 1891), WORD*search* CROSS e-book, 274.

school shootings, and we blame guns and mental illness but few blame the wickedness of mankind.

9 "The heart *is* deceitful above all *things,* And desperately wicked; Who can know it? Jeremiah 17:9 (NKJV)

Russian writer Alexandr Solzhenitsyn said:

"If only there were evil people somewhere, insidiously committing evil deeds, and it were necessary only to separate them from the rest of us and destroy them. But the line dividing good and evil cuts through the heart of every human being. And who is willing to destroy a piece of his own heart?"[127]

(2) The *Journey*.

4 *Then Jonah began to go through the city one day's walk* – does not mean that Jonah traveled into the city for a whole day before preaching. Instead, it means on the first day he entered the city he began preaching.

(3) The *Urgency*.

and he cried out and said, "Yet forty days..." - Our message is always urgent because we

---

[127] Submitted by Jeff Arthurs; quoted in: Bill Hybels, Making Life Work: Putting God's Wisdom into Action (InterVarsity, 1998), p. 204.

never know when we are going to die (Prov. 27:1/2 Cor. 6:2).

Oliver Wendell Holmes was asked why he had taken up the study of Greek at the age of 94. He said, "Well, my good sir, it's now or never."[128] They had only forty days, truth is there may be some here who have less then that before their life is over.

(4) The *Severity*.

and Nineveh will be overthrown – notice there is no call to repent or sliver of hope offered. It is not turn or burn but burn baby burn!

This is speaking of total destruction. It would not only be total but eternal! James Kennedy writes:

Forever and ever and ever. When you have been in hell a hundred billion, trillion eons of centuries, you will not have one less second to be there—to be lost forever. You will be in utter darkness, fleeing this way and that with never another mortal soul to converse with, never an angel to cross your track, turning this way and that, up and down one plane in every way, forever and ever lost, lost, shrieking out, lost, forever, where no echoes will ever mock your misery. Immortal soul, lost in an infinite darkness, flying on and on in a journey that

---

[128] He Still Moves Stones, Max Lucado, p. 205. Thomas Nelson 1999.

will only end when you will come to fold your wings upon the gravestone of God, forever.[129]

4. Nineveh's *Compliance*. 5-10

This reminds me of something I read:

So you're walking along the beach minding your own business, and all of a sudden this big fish slides himself up on shore, pukes all over, and slides back into the water. Out of the slime and fish parts and seaweed, a man drags himself out, struggles, and stands up — his clothes half digested, a piece of seaweed stuck to the side of his face. He looks at you, coughs up some seawater, clears his throat, and says, "Repent!" What would you do? I know what I'd do: I'd repent!"[130]

a. There was *Delivery* of God's Word. 3:2

2 "Arise, go to Nineveh the great city and proclaim to it the proclamation which I am going to tell you." – faith comes from God's Word (Rom. 10:17).

Boice notes:

---

[129] Kennedy, D. James. Why I Believe (p. 80). Thomas Nelson. Kindle Edition.
[130] Bramer, Stephen. The Bible Reader's Joke Book: This book contains a collection of over 2,000 jokes, puns, humorous stories and funny sayings related to the Bible: Arranged from Genesis to Revelation. (p. 184). Unknown. Kindle Edition.

Jonah preached what God had given him to preach, and it was highly effective. It was not a lengthy message, but that did not matter. It was not an intellectual message, but that did not matter either. Perhaps it was not even an eloquent message, but neither did that matter. All that was necessary was that it was God's message, preached and heard in the power of God's Holy Spirit."[131]

¹ I solemnly charge *you* in the presence of God and of Christ Jesus, who is to judge the living and the dead, and by His appearing and His kingdom: ² preach the word; be ready in season *and* out of season; reprove, rebuke, exhort, with great patience and instruction. ³ For the time will come when they will not endure sound doctrine; but *wanting* to have their ears tickled, they will accumulate for themselves teachers in accordance to their own desires, ⁴ and will turn away their ears from the truth and will turn aside to myths.
2 Timothy 4:1-4

We are living in days where personal opinion, the Constitution, the polls, the news media, and whatever has become our authority. All views must be accepted or at least respected except God's Word.

---

[131] An Expositional Commentary – The Minor Prophets, Volume 1: Hosea-Jonah, Paperback ed. (Grand Rapids, MI: Baker Books, 2006), WORDsearch CROSS e-book, 298.

Camp Quest West, just north of Sacramento, California, is no church camp. Designed for children of agnostics, atheists, freethinkers, and humanists, the mission of the camp is to:

"...promote respect for others with different viewpoints, values, and beliefs...we deplore efforts ... to seek to explain the world in supernatural terms and to look outside nature for salvation."

The weeklong experience includes crafts, campfires, and canoe trips, along with class sessions about evolution, the power of debate, and skepticism. Rick Rohrer the camp director says:

It's "a vacation from Judeo-Christian culture."

Edwin Kagin adds, "Kids come there and they cry. They say it's the first time in their life that they're able to express that they don't believe in God."

The camp ends with what director Chris Lindstrom calls "a competition for the kids to create their own religion that everyone can believe in and that will be good for all, for all time."[132]

---

[132] Richard Chin, "Camps sign up free thinkers," www.usatoday.com (4-11-2007), www.campquestwest.org, and Richard Chin, "Ungodly fun," Pioneer Press (9-9-04); submitted by Bill White, Paramount, California.

That is what America is becoming, a place where everyone seeks to be on vacation from God. It is our duty to confront this world with the Word of God!

b. There was *Dependency*. 5

⁵ Then the people of Nineveh believed in God – upwards to 150 times the Bible declares that salvation is by faith. That is always the issue – faith or unbelief (Jn. 16:8-11).

To say they believed also assumed they repented. Faith and repentance are two sides to one coin (Mt. 12:41).

Notice also it does not say they believed Jonah but they believed in God! We have to keep the focus where it belongs – on God not us.

Kendall notes, "Isn't this interesting? So the people of Nineveh believed God. It is not enough merely for men to believe us…men can believe in us and be lost. I never will forget a very powerful preacher who was once my pastor. This man, after he left the area and went on to another church, had many people who fell away from their profession of faith. It suggested how much they were followers of *him*…So it is not enough to believe in a man."[133]

---

[133] Jonah An Exposition, R. T. Kendall, p. 194. The Paternoster Press.

There is no substitute for faith in God (Heb. 11:6/Eph. 2:8-9).

A Canadian Press photo shows how one man from Havana, Cuba, tried to appease God's wrath. The man is lying on his back on a dirt road. Attached to his ankle is a chain several feet long. The other end of the chain is wrapped around a rock. The caption explains that the bearded man is inch by inch pulling the rock on a pilgrimage to a sanctuary dedicated to St. Lazarus.[134]

This man's faith is misguided, because it is placed in himself and what he can accomplish. It is a works salvation which is no salvation at all! Saving faith must be coupled with God's grace, it is completely unmerited and unearned.

c. There was a *Display* of humility. 5

and they called a fast and put on sackcloth from the greatest to the least of them – sackcloth was worn to express sorrow (1 Kings 20:31-32) repentance (Lam. 2:10/Joel 1:8/Esther 4:1-3) and mourning (2 Sam. 3:31). Here, it was an outward sign of an inwardly broken and contrite heart.

---

[134] Choice Contemporary Stories and Illustrations: For Preachers, Teachers, and Writers (Kindle Locations 114-116). Kindle Edition.

Pride refuses to put all of its trust in God, humility realizes it's only hope is in God. These people humbled themselves in the extreme. Macrina Wiederkehr notes:

Fasting makes me vulnerable and reminds me of my frailty. It reminds me to remember that if I am not fed I will die … Standing before God hungry, I suddenly know who I am. I am one who is poor, called to be rich in a way that the world does not understand. I am one who is empty, called to be filled with the fullness of God. I am one who is hungry, called to taste all the goodness that can be mine in Christ.[135]

d. The entire city was *Deeply* affected. 3:6-9

6 When the word reached the king of Nineveh, he arose from his throne, laid aside his robe from him, covered himself with sackcloth and sat on the ashes. 7 He issued a proclamation and it said, "In Nineveh by the decree of the king and his nobles: Do not let man, beast, herd, or flock taste a thing. Do not let them eat or drink water. 8 "But both man and beast must be covered with sackcloth; and let men call on God earnestly that each may turn from his wicked way and from the violence which is in his hands. 9 "Who knows, God may turn and relent and withdraw His burning anger so that

---

[135] Macrina Wiederkehr, A Tree Full of Angels (HarperOne, 2009), p. 36.

we will not perish." – this is remarkable! It effected everybody from the big shot to the little shot and those who ought to shot!

e. There was avoidance of *Doomsday*. 10

10 When God saw their deeds, that they turned from their wicked way, then God relented concerning the calamity which He had declared He would bring upon them. And He did not do it. – again notice God takes responsibility for the calamity that would have come upon them.

They took God's warning seriously, we preachers have been warning of a doomsday that is right around the corner – a Seven-year nightmare, but no one is too concerned about it.

On a balmy January Saturday morning, this year [2018] an alert warning of a nuclear doom was mistakenly sent to millions of people across the state of Hawaii.

"BALLISTIC MISSILE THREAT INBOUND TO HAWAII. SEEK IMMEDIATE SHELTER. THIS IS NOT A DRILL."

Those were the words that flashed on cell phones and televisions screens across the state, and it took 38 minutes before they put forth a correction that it was all a mistake. Somebody pushed the wrong button! The response was sheer panic![136]

But oddly enough God's warning of eternal wrath for all who reject Christ is met with a yawn. But it is no mistake to tell people that the end of their world could come at any moment – death or rapture is an any moment possibility.

Nineveh responded while the religious leaders of Jesus' day did not – how about us?

Note: There is the problem of God relenting. Can an immutable God really repent?

Charles Ryrie notes:

If God is immutable, how can it be said that He repents? (Gen. 6:6; Jon. 3:10). If there actually was a change in God Himself, then either He is not immutable or not sovereign or both. Most understand these verses as employing anthropomorphism; i.e., interpreting what is not human in human terms. In the unfolding revelation of God's plan there seems to be change. However, this can be said to be so only from the human viewpoint, for His eternal plan is unchanging, as is He.[137]

---

[136] Jelani Greenidge, PreachingToday.com; source: Dakin Andone, "From paradise to panic: Hawaii residents and vacationers run for cover, fearing missile attack" CNN (1-14-18).
[137] Charles Ryrie, Basic Theology: A Popular Systematic Guide to Understanding Biblical Truth, (Chicago: Moody Press, 1986), WORDsearch CROSS e-book, 43.

Wiersbe notes:

The phrase "God repented" might better be translated "God relented," that is, changed His course. From the human point of view, it looked like repentance, but from the divine perspective, it was simply God's response to man's change of heart. God is utterly consistent with Himself; it only appears that he is changing His mind. The Bible uses human analogies to reveal the divine character of God (Jer. 18:1-10).[138]

Let me try and illustrate this. As you know, I was born in Michigan, and because of Lake Michigan it can get very windy. Suppose I left my house as a boy and headed for the bus stop. It is windy and so I have to struggle to get there because I am walking against the wind. Then I realize I forgot my schoolbook, so I have to head back to the house, but this time the wind is at my back and I walk with ease. Notice it was not the wind that changed direction but me! God is immutable and He never changes, but when we repent, we are changing directions. God in a sense is not really responding to us, but we are responding to Him.

Con:

---

[138] Warren W. Wiersbe, The Bible Exposition Commentary – The Prophets, (Colorado Springs, CO: Victor, 2002), WORDsearch CROSS e-book, 385.

1. So we have Jonah getting a second chance, one he has taken advantage of.

2. Jonah had gone from running in the wrong direction, to being used to score a victory for the glory of God.

3. Have you ever heard the story of Wrong Way Roy? Roy Riegels, an All-American center for the University of California, Berkeley's Golden Bears who were facing Georgia Tech in the 1929 Rose Bowl. Midway through the second quarter, with Georgia Tech on offense on their own thirty, one of the Tech players fumbled the ball. Riegels alertly scooped it up and began to sprint toward the end zone, But there was one problem. It was the wrong end zone. If Roy had succeeded, he would have scored a touchdown for the opposing team. Riegels later told the Associated Press:

"I was running toward the sidelines when I picked up the ball. I started to my left toward Tech's goal. Somebody shoved me, and I bounded right off into a tackler. In pivoting to get away from him, I completely lost my bearings."

Fortunately, Benny Lom, one of his Cal teammates, caught up with Riegels before he got across the wrong goal line. Tech ended up scoring a safety before halftime and went into the locker rooms leading 2-0.

He told his coach, Nibs Price, during half-time in the locker room:

"Coach, I can't do it. I've ruined you, I've ruined myself, I've ruined the University of California. I couldn't face that crowd to save my life."

But Price told him, "Roy, get up and go back out there— the game is only half over."

Riegels did go back for the second half and turned in one of the most inspiring efforts in Rose Bowl history.[139]

God gave wrong way Jonah another chance – and I can testify He has also given Wrong Way Johnny a million and one chances!

Chapter Three

THE SECOND CHANCE CAN BE REJECTED

Jonah 4:1-11

Intro:

1. In Greek mythology Narcissus falls in love with his own reflection in a pool of water. He

---

[139] Laurie, Greg. A Fresh Look At the Book of Jonah: The hard to swallow truth about disobedience (Kindle Location 27). Allen David Books/Kerygma Inc. Kindle Edition.

loves the image so deeply he cannot leave the side of the pool. Thus we have Narcissism, speaking of one who is self-absorbed.

Joseph Stowell writes:

Narcissism is the notion that life should revolve around me and claims that I am the greatest entity in my personal universe. All that really matters are my rights, my privileges, my happiness and my prosperity. Other people are always secondary. Loving myself and looking out for "number one" are all that matters...The result of self-dominated thinking is the destruction and alienation from others and God as we lock out everyone else and barricade ourselves within a ghetto of one!"

In Woody Allen's movie Scoop, a character who used to believe in Judaism but now has converted to another religion describes his shift in belief. Sid Waterman says, "I was born into the Hebrew persuasion, but when I got older I converted to narcissism."[140]

2. Jonah was a prophet of God but somewhere along the way, he was converted to narcissism and became a prophet of self. The sad truth, we are never told whether he converted back to a prophet of God or not. If not, he let his Second Chance slip through his fingers.

---

[140] Bob, Steven. Jonah and the Meaning of Our Lives: A Verse-by-Verse Contemporary Commentary (p. 195). The Jewish Publication Society. Kindle Edition.

3. The Second Chance can be Rejected.

Trans: Perhaps Jonah, and for sure a future generation of Ninevehites who refuse God's offer of a second chance. Jonah 4:1-11

I. FIRST, THE SECOND CHANCE IS REQUIRED. 1:1-16

II. FURTHERMORE, THE SECOND CHANCE RECEIVED. 1:17-3:10

III. FINALLY, THE SECOND CHANCE CAN BE REJECTED. 4:1-11

A. First, Jonah's *Languished*. 4:1-15

1. Due to selfish *Pride*. 4:1

[1] But it greatly displeased Jonah and he became angry – the verb anger comes from a root which means "to glow hot."

In his mind his reputation was now damaged, he went from Hero to Heel. He is self-absorbed. As John Butler put it:

"Jonah's displeasure was rooted and grounded in selfishness. To be displeased with God is one of the hallmarks of selfishness. When you find a person who is unhappy with the way God is doing things or wants things done, you have just found a selfish person. It is either self or God."[141] See Luke 9:23

Step back and take note of the personal pronouns:

¹ But Jonah was greatly displeased and became angry. ² He prayed to the LORD, "O LORD, is this not what **I** said when **I** was still at home? That is why **I** was so quick to flee to Tarshish. **I** knew that you are a gracious and compassionate God, slow to anger and abounding in love, a God who relents from sending calamity. ³ Now, O LORD, take away **my** life, for it is better for **me** to die than to live." Jonah 4:1-3 (NIV)

Jonah did not care what was best for the people of Nineveh or God or anybody else – it is all about what is best for me!

Selfishness is in reality seeking a restraining order against God! We do not want Him or His plans or His ways.

In May 2016 an Israeli man petitioned for a restraining order against God. The plaintiff, identified as Mr. David Shoshan, represented himself at a court hearing in Haifa, a port city in the north of Israel.

---

[141] Jonah, The Parochial Prophet, p. 183, Published by LBC Publications, 1994.

The report noted that God was not present to defend himself. (Of course, God was present but didn't feel a need to defend himself). David told the court that God had been treating him "harshly and not nicely." David also explained that he had made several attempts to contact police to report God's alleged crimes, and that patrol cars had been sent to his house on 10 occasions. Police advised David to try taking out a restraining order. The request for a restraining order was denied by the presiding Judge Ahsan Canaan, who said the request was "delusional" and that the petitioner required help from sources outside of the court.[142]

We have a lot of delusional Christians who think they can keep God out of their lives and run it their way.

2. His selfish *Prayers*. 2-3

a. His lapse back into *Carnality.*

2 He prayed to the LORD and said, "Please LORD, was not this what I said while I was still in my own country? – in other words he admits his sinful attitude that he had when he left for Joppa.

---

[142] Adapted from Elsa Vulliamy, "Man seeks restraining order against God," Independent (5-6-16).

But I thought Jonah repented in the raging sea? Was that not real repentance? Yes! But we can lapse back into sin! We cannot confess sin, repent, and get back to walking with God and think that is the end of it. We still have an old sin nature, we have to maintain our obedience (Mt. 26:41/Gal. 5:16/Eph. 6:12/2 Cor. 10:4-5).

This life is a warfare and we are never done fighting the self monster! Barry Merritt of Ohio shared this:

When we lived in St. Petersburg, Florida, we would go to the beach. It was always hard to relax and have a good time with our children, though, because there were too many threats: jellyfish, stingrays, sharks, undertow.
One time we had some relatives that came to St. Petersburg and brought their boat with them. We decided to go out to an island a couple of miles offshore called Egmont Key. We had a great time because we didn't think we had to worry about the normal threats. The water was blue, the sand was white. We swam with our children carefree in the Gulf of Mexico. A few days later we were telling some friends about our wonderful day. Being more familiar with the area, they informed us we had been swimming in one of the most shark-infested areas around! We were in danger, but completely oblivious to it.[143]

---

[143] Barry Merritt, Toledo, Ohio.

We need to be aware that we live among many threats – the world-system; self; and Satan are all wanting to take over.

b. He even had a selfish *Philosophy*.

Therefore in order to forestall this I fled to Tarshish, for I knew that You are a gracious and compassionate God, slow to anger and abundant in lovingkindness, and one who relents concerning calamity.- It is amazing how we want God to be gracious to us but then begrudge Him showing grace to those we do not like.

Many of us have no problem *receiving* grace, but have a problem with *showing* grace to others. He had good theology, he knew God was patient, gracious, and loving, but he had reshaped it into a selfish philosophy. Good theology is God loves everybody and is gracious to all, not giving them what they deserve in this life; but a bad philosophy takes that and twists it to mean, God's grace can only go so far, it must have limits, especially toward those who have done me wrong!

We must not let those illegal aliens stay in our country – they have broken the law! They do not deserve to stay and I will vote against anybody who offers them amnesty!

But many of them are criminals! I know but for a reason known only to God, He is patient with them. Keep in mind within about 40 years from Jonah's time, the Assyrians would take Israel into captivity. As one put it:

It isn't hard to relate to Jonah's problem. If God had wiped out Hitler, or Stalin or Osama Bin Laden when they were young, the world would have been spared unspeakable evil and suffering. But God let them live! Why? Because He is "gracious and compassionate ... slow to anger and abounding in love." That was Jonah's complaint.... Grace means that God may bless people who have wronged you, people from whose sins you have suffered. When that happens, you may find yourself asking, "Why doesn't God give them what they deserve?" Sometimes God seems to bless the wrong people. His grace seems misdirected.[144]

The truth is there is a Jonah in all of us, dare I say a Hitler as well? It is called the old sin nature whose righteous deeds are like a filthy rag (Isa. 64:6/Rom. 3:10-18).

c. He had a quitters *Mentality*.

3 "Therefore now, O LORD, please take my life from me, for death is better to me than life." – It's amazing that the book doesn't end with verse three! I love to watch Westerns, one of

---

[144] Smith, Colin S.. Jonah: Navigating a God-centered Life (Kindle Locations 904-905). Christian Focus Publications. Kindle Edition.

the things I noticed that if it's an old western it always has two big words at the end of it –THE END. I often wonder why they did that, did they think we are so stupid we did not know that the movie ended? I can see my wife walking into the room finding me staring at a blank screen. Hey, what are you doing? Oh, I am just waiting for the movie to end!

If I was God, I would have answered Jonah's prayer and just put up a grave marker with two words on it – THE END! The amazing grace of it all is that it is never the end in our relationship with God. Jonah is acting like a spoiled brat but notice how God doesn't zap him but patiently endures. Martin Luther notes:

"We must note first of all how wondrous God is in His saints, lest we be tempted to judge and condemn them thoughtlessly because of any of their actions. This work here may be evil— as indeed it is. But for all of that, I must not despise and reject the person. For if we regard Jonah in this act, we must agree that his actions are surely wrong; for God Himself punishes him. And yet he is God's dear child. He chats so uninhibitedly with God as though he were not in the least afraid of Him— as indeed he is not; he confides in Him as in a father" (AE 19: 92).[145]

---

[145] Various, Authors. The Lutheran Study Bible (Kindle Locations 233886-233890). Concordia Publishing House. Kindle Edition.

His threat is, it is my way or the high way!
Lord if you do not do it my way I will just quit!
How many just quit when things don't go their
way. I do not like the way this marriage is
going so I will just quit; I do not like the way
things are going on my job, I will get another;
I do not like the way they do things in my
church so I will find another one.
Of course, some of God's finest servants
wanted to just end it all and quit:

- Moses—Numbers 11:15
- Elijah—1 Kings 19:4
- Job and Jeremiah were weary of life and lamented the day of their births.

We may quit on God, but the amazing thing is that God never quits on us (Heb. 13:5-6).

3. His selfish *Pouting.* 4-5, 9

a. A Searching question.

⁴ The LORD said, "Do you have good reason to be angry?" – is assumes a negative answer. He is asking Jonah to think about his response. If you search your heart you will know that your anger is totally unjustified.

As one put it:

Like a physician probing a wound before he medicates it to bring about its healing, so God probes the heart of Jonah with a soul searching question. What condescension it was for God to deal so patiently with Jonah. God could have squashed Jonah to a damp spot on the desert sands outside of Nineveh with one justified stomp of His holy foot…But God is exactly what Jonah knew God to be "slow to anger, and of great kindness (v. 3).[146]

Billy Graham said, "I'll never forget when she announced what she wanted on her gravestone, and those who have so graciously visited her gravesite at the Billy Graham Library have seen that she got her way. Long before Ruth became bedridden, she was driving along a highway through a construction site. Carefully following the detours and mile-by-mile cautionary signs, she came to the last one that said, "End of Construction. Thank You for Your Patience." She arrived home that day chuckling and told the family about the postings. "When I die," she said, "I want that engraved on my stone."[147]

I have heard over and over again about the patience of Job, that cannot even compare with the patience of God!

b. A Sitting down to see if God would destroy the city.

---

[146] Jonah, The Parochial Prophet, p. 193, Published by LBC Publications, 1994.
[147] Graham, Billy. Where I Am: Heaven, Eternity, and Our Life Beyond (p. 178). Thomas Nelson. Kindle Edition.

5 Then Jonah went out from the city and sat east of it. - Jonah just ignores God's question and continues in his stubborn rebellion!

Another thing to be noted is that those in Nineveh needed follow-up and discipleship. They are just spiritual babies and need guidance and teaching but Jonah is too self-focused to care about their spiritual well-being.

He has dug in his heels; he is not only rebellious but stubbornly rebellious. It is not wise to persist in our rebellious ways. An epitaph on the gravestone of an army mule:

Here lies Maggie,
who in her time kicked two captains,
four lieutenants,
ten sergeants,
fifty privates,
and one bomb.[148]

T bottom line is that God is not going to abandon His truth for Jonah's distorted reasoning. He can sit on that hill till he grows old and dies but the city of Nineveh has been spared!

---

[148] Bramer, Stephen. The Bible Reader's Joke Book: This book contains a collection of over 2,000 jokes, puns, humorous stories and funny sayings related to the Bible: Arranged from Genesis to Revelation. (p. 143). Unknown. Kindle Edition.

When the infidel Robert G. Ingersoll was delivering his lectures against Christ and the Bible, his oratorical ability usually assured him of a large crowd. One night after an inflammatory speech in which he severely attacked man's faith in the Savior, he dramatically took out his watch and said:

"I'll give God a chance to prove that He exists and is almighty. I challenge Him to strike me dead within 5 minutes!" First there was silence, then people became uneasy. Some left the hall, unable to take the nervous strain of the occasion, and one woman fainted. At the end of the allotted time, the atheist exclaimed derisively: "See! There is no God. I am still very much alive!"

After the lecture a young fellow said to a Christian lady, "Well, Ingersoll certainly proved something tonight!" Her reply was memorable. "Yes he did, He proved God isn't taking orders from atheists tonight."[149]

God is not taking orders from Jonah or anybody else for that matter, whether it be a believer or an atheist.

c. Making a little Shelter to give him shade from the sun.

---

[149] Jim Wilson, Fresh Sermons, WORDsearch CROSS e-book, Under: "Games People Play".

There he made a shelter for himself and sat under it in the shade until he could see what would happen in the city. – this would be made of twigs and whatever could be found. These shelters were built for Cattle (Gen. 33:170, travelers (Lev. 23:43), religious pilgrims (Neh. 8:15-17), or for those guarding crops (Job 27:18)

B. Second, God's *Lesson*. 4:6-11

1. A *Demonstration*. 6-8

a. Jonah's plant *Withered*

⁶ And when the leaves of the shelter withered in the heat... Jonah 4:6 (TLB)

b. The Lord prepared a *Wee* little plant. 6

(1) It was *Sent* by God Himself.

⁶ *So the LORD God appointed* – again we see God's providence in every page of this little book. God is not just responsible for this Wee little plant, but also the Worm that took it away, as well as the scorching Wind.

I read the story of a couple who endured the tragic loss of their teenage son through a road accident. In their sorrow, they reached out to a pastor who told them, "Sometimes even God makes mistakes." That pastor is doing more harm than, if he just told the truth, that God was behind the death of their son, even though we cannot not understand why, He in His wisdom does what He does.

Alan Redpath, who was the pastor of Moody church in Chicago, suffered a stroke which caused much suffering. He writes:

There is no circumstance, no trouble, no testing, that can ever touch me until, first of all, it has gone past God and past Christ, right through to me. If it has come that far, it has come with a great purpose, which I may not understand at the moment. But I refuse to panic, as I lift up my eyes to Him and accept it as a coming from the throne of God for some great purpose of blessing to my own heart.[150]

(2) The plant started out *Small*.

⁶ So the LORD God appointed a plant – The NET note observes:

The noun קִיקָיוֹן (*qiqayon*, "plant") has the suffixed ending יִ- which denotes a diminutive (see *IBHS* 92 e5.7b), so it can be nuanced "little plant." For the probable reason that the narrator used the diminutive form here, see the note on "little" in v. 10.[151]

---

[150] Smith, Colin S.. Jonah: Navigating a God-centered Life (Kindle Locations 1136-1138). Christian Focus Publications. Kindle Edition.
[151] *NET Bible*, First ed. (Richardson, TX: Biblical Studies Press, 1996), WORD*search* CROSS e-book, Under: "Chapter 4".

(3) It grew *Supernaturally*.

and it grew up over Jonah – this is not a normal growth! As one put it:

'Miracle-Gro' never produced anything like this! It was a miracle vine. Picture a time-lapse video, showing the growth of a plant from seedling to full maturity in a matter of minutes. That's how this vine appeared. It was a miraculous gift from the Lord.[152]

(4) It provided *Shade*.

to be a shade over his head to deliver him from his discomfort. – notice this was not due to any merit on Jonah's part. Likewise, none of us deserve any blessing from God. When God blesses us it should encourage humility not pride. It reminds me of Winston Churchill, we watched the movie Darkest Hour the other day, it was a great movie about Winston Churchill. One of his political opponents was Clement Atlee, Churchill never liked the man. Once someone told him that Atlee was a wonderful humble man." Churchill replied, "Of course, he has a lot to be humble about!" Truth is we all do.

(5) It made Jonah *Slap happy*!

---

[152] Smith, Colin S.. Jonah: Navigating a God-centered Life (Kindle Locations 1107-1108). Christian Focus Publications. Kindle Edition.

And Jonah was extremely happy about the plant. – he was sitting pretty, a slang for doing very nicely. He was back in his comfort zone.

John Ortberg writes:

Too much comfort is dangerous. Literally. Researchers at the University of California, Berkeley, did an experiment some time ago that involved introducing an amoeba into a perfectly stress-free environment: ideal temperature, optimal concentration of moisture, constant food supply. The amoeba had an environment to which it had to make no adjustment whatsoever.
So you would guess this was one happy little amoeba. Whatever it is that gives amoebas ulcers and high blood pressure was gone.
Yet, oddly enough, it died.[153]

Self-centered comfort is in reality a killer – it is to focus on God's blessings without focusing on the source of it.

Hawkins makes good application:

Each of us should ask the question, "What is my vine?" In what do I trust and find joy?...Some of us wonder why we used to be happy in the Lord Jesus and now we are angry. Some of us feel He has left us. Could it be that

---

[153] "If You Want to Walk on Water, You've Got to Get Out of the Boat" by John Ortberg, p. 56.

we started delighting more in the vine than in the Lord Jesus? Could it be that He sent a worm to show us that it is not the temporal but the eternal that is really important?[154]

c. The Lord prepared a *Worm*. 7

7 But God appointed a worm when dawn came the next day and it attacked the plant and it withered. – let's never forget that every blessing we experience is due to God's gracious hand. He owes us nothing and our attitude should be like that of Job.

20 Then Job arose and tore his robe and shaved his head, and he fell to the ground and worshiped. 21 He said, "Naked I came from my mother's womb, And naked I shall return there. The LORD gave and the LORD has taken away. Blessed be the name of the LORD." 22 Through all this Job did not sin nor did he blame God. Job 1:20-22

I like the way J. Vernon McGee comments on that verse:

Here is a viewpoint of life and a philosophy of life that Christians need today toward material things. You and I came into this world with nothing. We were naked as jaybirds when we came into this world. And we are going to

---

[154] Meeting the God of the Second Chance, Jonah, O. S. Hawkins, p. 112, Loizeaux Brothers Publications, 190.

leave the world the same way. Remember the old bromide, "There are no pockets in a shroud"? My friend, you can't take anything with you. The story is told that years ago all the relatives were standing outside the bedroom door of the patriarch of a very wealthy family. They were waiting for the old man to die and for the family lawyer to come out. When he came, he announced to them all that the father had died. Immediately one of the more greedy ones asked, "How much did he leave?" And the lawyer replied, "He left it all. He didn't take anything with him."
That is the way it will be with all of us. It makes no difference how many deeds you have or how strong your safety deposit box may be, what you accumulate or how much insurance you have. When you go and when I go, we're going just like we came into this world. It is very important for us to get this into our philosophy of life. You may be living today in an expensive home, or you may be living in a hovel. You may have a big bank account, or you may not have anything to count at all. You may have a safety deposit box filled with stocks and bonds, or you may not even have a safety deposit box. It makes no difference who you are. We're all going to leave the same way we came into this world. Whatever you have, you are simply a steward of it. Really, in the final analysis, it does not belong to you, does it?[155]

---

[155] J. Vernon McGee, *Thru The Bible with J. Vernon McGee*, (Nashville,

Jonah did not deserve that plant, it was an unearned and undeserved gift from God, and thus he had no right to complain about its removal.

d. Then God-prepared a scorching east Wind. 8

8 When the sun came up God appointed a scorching east wind, and the sun beat down on Jonah's head so that he became faint and begged with all his soul to die, saying, "Death is better to me than life." – Jonah could star in a movie *Death Wish* – I, II, & II!

These winds are brutal; one feels like he is suffocating with particles of sand blinding one's vision, it could cause a deadly sunstroke.

All of this reminds me of something John Newton wrote:

I asked the Lord that I might grow
In faith, and love, and every grace;
Might more of his salvation know,
And seek, more earnestly, his face...
I hoped that in some favored hour,
At once he'd answer my request;
And by His love's constraining power,
Subdue my sins, and give me rest.

TN: Thomas Nelson, 1983), WORD*search* CROSS e-book, Under: "Chapter 1".

Instead of this, he made me feel
The hidden evils of my heart;
And let the angry powers of hell
Assault my soul in every part.
Yea more, with his own hand he seemed
Intent to aggravate my woe;
Crossed all the fair designs I schemed,
Blasted my gourds, and laid me low.

"Lord, why is this?" I trembling cried,
"Wilt Thou pursue Thy worm to death?"
"Tis in this way," the Lord replied,
"I answer prayer for grace and faith.
"These inward trials I employ,
From self, and pride, to set thee free;
And break thy schemes of earthly joy,
That thou may'st seek thy all in Me."[156]

2. A *Declaration*. 9-11

a. God's *Challenge*.

9 Then God said to Jonah, "Do you have good reason to be angry about the plant?" – how ridiculous to be grieved over the destruction of a plant but not about the destruction of an entire city. He actually preferred that the city be destroyed and the plant be spared! Talk about mixed up priorities. God was trying get Jonah to see the truth, but he seems to have missed the point of the plant, worm, and

---

[156] John Newton, Olney Hymns, 1779.

scorching wind. It was designed to explain to him how much God loves people but all Jonah could focus on his was losses. Reminds me of a man who was demonstrating the effectiveness of a certain window cleaner. He smeared some butter on a window and then used the cleaner to wipe it off. He then asked if anyone had any questions. On lady raised her hand and asked, "Yes, how much butter are we supposed to use?" She like, Jonah missed the point of the demonstration.

b. Jonah's continual *Contempt*.

And he said, "I have good reason to be angry, even to death."

Jonah reminds me of the boy whose mother made him say five hundred times 'I'm a disobedient boy.' But he got even with her. When he got to his room he said five hundred times 'No I ain't'"

c. Jonah's shallow *Compassion*.

Then the LORD said, "You had compassion on the plant for which you did not work and which you did not cause to grow, which came up overnight and perished overnight. – we have a lot of people with shallow compassion. You can see a 5 minute commercial about the cruelty to animals, but that same person could care less about those little babies being slaughtered in abortion.

Some time ago, I shot a deer during hunting season and had to follow that deer for a long way before I found him. I went down hills, up hills, stumbled over rocks, branches, and things I did not know what it was. When I found it, it was still standing but eventually fell over dead. I had to drag that deer a long way to get it home, uphill, tall grass, and stopping every few minutes gasping for air! I shared that with my mother and she winced, "Oh that poor deer!" I thought, mom this is your own son, I about had a heart attack out there and you are concerned about the deer! It is ok to be concerned about animals and, I suppose, even plants, but they are not in the same category with people created in the image of God. Of course, Jonah's compassion was not for that plant but for his own creature comforts.

d. God's *Compassion* for His creation.

(1) He cares about the Lost.

[11]"Should I not have compassion on Nineveh, the great city in which there are more than 120,000 persons who do not know the difference between their right and left hand – God the Father, Son, and Holy Spirit rejoice when just one person is saved. All of the angels in heaven rejoice when just one sinner is saved. How much more when 120,000 respond!

PS: Some take the 120,000 people who could not tell their right hand from their left is a reference to young children, but it is likely a description of people who have lost their ability to discern right from wrong.

We also should have enough compassion to care about whether people in our own city are saved.

Jonah built a little booth,
A shelter from the heat.
A gourd-vine grew, protection from
The wind, that on him beat

Jonah rejoiced, exceedingly glad
For tis convient gourd –
Especially since this comfort was
Provided by the Lord!

"I thank Thee, Lord; Thou has been good,
To my dear wife and me;
We're glad were in a peaceful land
Of great prosperity.

It makes us feel so good
This little bungalow
The kitchenette, the living room
The rug, so soft, you know.

And fundamentalists are we,
My children, wife and I
So thankful that we're saved by grace,

Secure until we die.

What did you say? Oh, Nineveh!
Well, that's another thing.
Right now we want to Praise our God.
Were sheltered 'neath His wings!"

Thus fundamental Jonah's too
The Lord their praises tell.
While Nineveh goes to hell!"

Of course, this is not designed to be a guilt trip or teach that we are the author of anyone's faith. We can only plant and water, but God alone causes the increase.

(2) He cares about the Livestock.

as well as many animals? – I think my mother probably appreciates this verse! And yet, it is certainly not putting animals in the same class as people created in the image of God.

Trans: God is using Jonah's shallow compassion and lack of concern about the people of Nineveh to show Jonah the absurdity of being angry with God's compassion for the people of Nineveh.

One of the things that this points out is the foolishness of thinking we know better than God. We don't! Jonah sin was that of playing God and criticizing God for being God. Jonah is not the hero of this book, God is, the one we want to be like is Jehovah not Jonah!

Con:

1. So we have a Second Chance Required because of our failures; and a Second Chance can be Received only because of God's mercy and grace; and a Second Chance can be Rejected.

2. The God of the Second Chance.

3. One thing for sure when we become narcissistic, focused only on getting our way we are effectively blocking God from doing anything in our lives.

 An example of a narcissistic life is known in the life of Don Juan. In Spanish it is Don Juan, also known in Italian, as Don Giovanni. Mozart's opera Don Giovanni tells the story of this self-centered nobleman who seduces whomever he pleases, treating men and women as mere playthings. He cares only about his own pleasure and entertainment. He cares nothing about the impact of his actions on other people.

In the opening scene of the opera, he is attempting to seduce Donna Anna, the daughter of the Commendatore. Donna Anna cries for help, and the Commendatore comes to his daughter's aid. He fights a duel with Don Giovanni, who kills him. The Commendatore's death does not trouble Don Giovanni at all. He continues to seduce and scheme. Later in the opera Don Giovanni taunts a statue of the Commendatore in the cemetery and afterwards he orders his servant to invite the statue to join him for dinner. That evening Don Giovanni hears a knock on his door. The statue of the Commendatore enters and offers Don Giovanni a last opportunity to repent of his narcissistic sins. Don Giovanni refuses. The Commendatore grabs hold of Don Giovanni and drags him down into hell.[157]

For the future Ninevites who, unlike the generation in Jonah's day, would reject God's second chance they would indeed be thrust into hell. For Jonah, if he remained self-absorbed, thus rejecting God's second chance, he would not end up in hell, but the remainder of his earthly life would be a sort of hell on earth – separated from God's will for his life.

Gaebelein comments:

"Jonah is silenced; he could not reply. The last words belong to Jehovah, who thus demonstrated in His infinite compassion He embraces not Israel alone, but all His creation, the Gentile world and even animal creation."

---

[157] Bob, Steven. Jonah and the Meaning of Our Lives: A Verse-by-Verse Contemporary Commentary (pp. 195-196). The Jewish Publication Society. Kindle Edition.

Was Jonah persuaded? We are not told but it doesn't really matter because one "greater than Jonah" is our example.

Gospel Presentation:

Let me ask you one of the most important questions you will ever ponder.

Have you come to a place in your life where you know for certain that if you died you would go to heaven?

The only answer to that question is, yes, no, or I don't know. Take a moment and think about it. A follow up question would be:'

If you were standing before God right now and He were to ask, "Why should I let you into my perfect heaven?"

What do you think you would say? You might say, "I go to church. I try to live a good life. I try to keep God's law." Such responses are sincere, and I appreciate your honesty. Most would probably say, "I don't know what I would say." Well, would you like to know? Then read the following carefully.

God Really Does Love You

"For God so loved the world, (put your name here), that He gave His only begotten Son, that whoever believes in Him should not perish but have everlasting life" (John 3:16).

It is natural to question this claim; we tend to wonder how God could love us with all of our problems and hang-ups, yes, you can say it – with all of our sins. My wife and I have had two children. When they were born they did nothing for us! And after they were born, for the first several months they kept us up all hours of the night; we had to change their diapers and feed them. I think most of you know what I'm talking about. However, we did love them. Why? I suppose it was because we had something to do with them being in this world. They are our children; they even looked a little like us – poor kids! You need to realize that God is the one who had everything to do with your coming into this world. Without God you would not even exist! He is the Creator and Sustainer of life. He, in fact, created you in His image and loves you even though you have done nothing to deserve it.

So What's a Fella to Do?

Have you ever felt that your life lacked purpose and meaning? Have these thoughts ever crossed your mind:

- Where did I come from?
- Why am I here?

- Where am I going?

God knows the answer to these questions. He created you with a definite purpose in mind.

"The thief does not come except to steal, and to kill, and to destroy. I have come that they may have life, and that they may have it more abundantly" (John 10:10).

An abundant life is a life of purpose, meaning, and fulfillment. That is what God offers you. This brings up an unavoidable question—what happened! If He loves us and has this great purpose for our life, then why are both concepts so foreign to us? The answer is both profound and very simple.

Sin Separates!

We are all sinners, "for all have sinned and fall short of the glory of God" (Rom. 3:22). We are a sinner by birth. God created Adam and Eve and put them in a garden with only one commandment; they were not to eat of a certain tree. They disobeyed God by taking a bite, and thus they sinned. Now what kind of babies are two sinful people capable of having? It is the law of biogenesis—like produces like. This is why there is no need to teach children how to tell a lie, but only to teach them positive things like telling the truth. They know how to lie naturally!

The reason for that is that we are all born with a sin nature inherited from Adam.

"Therefore, just as through one man sin entered the world, and death through sin, and thus death spread to all men, because all sinned" (Rom. 5:12).

We are also sinners by behavior. Have you not sinned? The Bible commands us to love God with all our heart, mind, and soul. Have you always done that? Have you ever done that? Have you ever told a lie? Have you ever wanted to? God not only looks at our deeds but at our desires. The Bible clearly declares we have all sinned.

So What?

Here is the answer to the so-what question.

"For the wages of sin is death, but the gift of God is eternal life in Christ Jesus our Lord" (Rom. 6:23).

What we have earned from our sin is death. Death means separation.

- There is spiritual death—the separation of the spirit/soul from God. "And the LORD God commanded the man, saying, 'Of every tree of the garden you may freely eat; but of the tree of the knowledge of good and evil you shall not eat, for in the day that you eat of it you shall surely die'" (Gen. 2:16–17). The day they ate of it they did not physically die; that took place many years later. But God said *in the day* you eat of it you will die. They died spiritually that very day.

- There is also physical death—the separation of the spirit/soul from the body. "And as it is appointed for men to die once, but after this the judgment" (Heb. 9:27). The fact that everybody dies physically is proof positive that everyone is spiritually dead. If we were not sinners, we would not die. The statistics are rather impressive; one out of every one person dies!

- If you die physically while you are spiritually dead, you will die eternally. Eternal death is the eternal separation of the spirit/soul/body from God's goodness, grace, mercy, and blessings. It is to be fully conscious and live in a place the Bible calls the lake of fire. "Then Death and Hades were cast into the lake of fire. This is the second death. And anyone not found written in the Book of Life was cast into the lake of fire" (Rev. 20:14–15).

Question: How can you say one moment that God loves me and then in the next that He condemns me?

Well let us imagine putting on a judge's robe and sitting on the bench. Then the unthinkable happens. Your son, whom you love very much, is brought before you, guilty of a capital offense! The penalty for his crime is death, and the evidence is clear as to his guilt. Would you sentence him to death? If you were a just judge, you would, not because you no longer love him, but in spite of your great love for him. God is holy, righteous, and just, as well as a God of love. This looks like bad news! However, the very word *gospel* means good news, so where is this good news?

Jesus Christ Is God

"In the beginning was the Word, and the Word was with God, and the Word was God" (John 1:1).

This is a great mystery, but the Bible teaches that God became God/man. "And the Word became flesh and dwelt among us, and we beheld His glory, the glory as of the only begotten of the Father, full of grace and truth" (John 1:14).

Jesus Christ the Substitute

The Lord Jesus Christ lived a perfect life and then died in your place. "But God demonstrates His own love toward us, in that while we were still sinners, Christ died for us" (Rom. 5:8 NKJV).

Let us put our judge robe back on for a minute. Imagine after sentencing your boy to be executed, taking off your robe and then voluntarily offering to die in his place. That would make you just and loving at the same time. That is what Jesus Christ actually did for us. We do not understand all of this but must accept it by faith. I do not understand electricity, but I still do not live in the dark. I do not understand how the digestive system works, but I still eat. I do not understand how a brown cow eats green grass and produces white milk. You do not have to understand everything to be saved—just that you are a sinner and that Jesus Christ died for your sin.

He Is Not Here, He Has Risen

"For I delivered to you first of all that which I also received: that Christ died for our sins according to the Scriptures, and that He was buried, and that He rose again the third day according to the Scriptures, and that He was seen by Cephas, then by the twelve. After that He was seen by over five hundred brethren at once, of whom the greater part remain to the present, but some have fallen asleep" (1 Cor. 15:3–6).

By rising from the dead, He proved that He paid for all of our sins. If He had not, death would have held Him. It also proved that He had no sin of His own. If He had, He would have stayed dead like everybody else.

One Way Only

We have all seen *One Way Only* signs, and so it is with the way of salvation. There is only one person who can save. "Jesus said to him, 'I am the way, the truth, and the life. No one comes to the Father except through Me'" (John 14:6).

You can line up every one of us on the West Coast with plans to swim to Hawaii, and no doubt, some would swim a lot farther than others. Nevertheless, we would all have one thing in common: nobody would make it! It is impossible for anybody to swim from the West Coast to Hawaii. And it is just as impossible for sinful man to make his way to a Holy God on his own without experiencing God's wrath. What one needs is a boat to get them from the West Coast to Hawaii. Moreover, the only salvation boat is the Lord Jesus Christ. That Jesus is the only way to be saved is as true as $2 + 2 = 4$. There is only one answer to that equation, and there is only one way to be saved.

"Nor is there salvation in any other, for there is no other name under heaven given among men by which we must be saved" (Acts 4:12).

Facts

These are only facts. Giving mental assent to these facts is not enough to save anyone. It is not enough to give intellectual assent to these facts. We must believe and thus receive Christ.

"But as many as received Him, to them He gave the right to become children of God, to those who believe in His name" (John 1:12).

Faith

Facts must be wedded to faith. So, what do we mean when we say believe or place your faith in Christ?

Faith involves mind, emotion, and will.

Years ago, a tightrope walker named Charles Blondin, went across Niagara Falls, walking on a wire. He went back and forth. He even filled a wheelbarrow with bricks and took that across. A crowd gathered, and he asked one of them, "Do you believe I could do that with you?" The man agreed that he could. Then Blondin said, "Hop on in, and I'll carry you across." The man said, "No way!" You see, he did not really believe. He believed in his mind that Blondin could take him across; he wanted him to in his emotions, but he would not commit himself to Blondin and trust him to take him across. Saving faith involves our mind, emotion, and will.

Amazing Grace

You likely have heard the song, "Amazing Grace." We are saved by grace through faith in Jesus Christ. Now faith is not a work—faith is to believe in the work of another. "For by grace you have been saved through faith, and that not of yourselves; it is the gift of God, not of works, lest anyone should boast" (Eph. 2:8–9).

Dr. Gerstner: "Christ has done everything necessary for his salvation. Nothing now stands between the sinner and God but the sinner's good works. Nothing can keep him from Christ but his delusion that he does not need Him—that he has good works of his own that can satisfy God. If men will only be convinced that all their righteousness is as filthy rags; if men will see that there is none that does good, no, not one; if men will see that all are shut up under sin—then there will be nothing to prevent their everlasting salvation. All they need is need. All they must have is nothing. All that is required is acknowledged guilt. But alas, sinners cannot part from their virtues. They are imaginary, but they are real to them. So grace becomes unreal. The real grace of God they spurn in order to hold on to the illusory virtues of their own. Their eyes fixed on a mirage; they will not drink real water. They die of thirst in the midst of an ocean of grace."

Repentance is a synonym for faith; it is like heads and tails of *one* coin. Repentance is not making a vow you will stop sinning, nor is it a change of life. You cannot stop sinning or change your life until God saves you! I have fished most of my life and I have never cleaned a fish before I caught it. Repentance is a *change of mind*, about who you are, a sinner; and about the Lord Jesus Christ, the only one who can save you based on His death, burial, and resurrection.

Good Enough Is Not Good Enough

The religious leaders of Jesus' day prayed three times a week, fasted twice a week, never missed going to the house of worship, and memorized the Old Testament (Luke 18:9–12). Yet, Jesus said that if you are not more righteous then they, you are not going to make it!

"For I say to you, that unless your righteousness exceeds the righteousness of the scribes and Pharisees, you will by no means enter the kingdom of heaven (Matt. 5:20).

Then he says something rather startling:

"Therefore you shall be perfect, just as your Father in heaven is perfect" (Matt. 5:48).

Did you know Jesus said it takes perfect righteousness to get to heaven? We all know that nobody is perfect! How then can we be perfectly righteous before a perfectly righteous God?

"For He made Him who knew no sin to be sin for us, that we might become the righteousness of God in Him" (2 Cor. 5:21).

The truth is, there is only one person who lived a perfect life, and that was Jesus Christ. You see, the good news is that not only did Jesus die on the cross in our place, to offer us forgiveness of all our sins, He also offers us His perfect righteousness, placed on our account! The only sin Jesus ever knew was ours; the only righteousness we will ever know is His.

Never the Same!

Salvation is not an external thing. When you receive Jesus Christ as your Savior, He makes you a new creature within!

"Therefore, if anyone is in Christ, he is a new creation; old things have passed away; behold, all things have become new" (2 Cor. 5:17). And the Holy Spirit takes up permanent residence within you.

"And because you are sons, God has sent forth the Spirit of His Son into your hearts, crying out, 'Abba, Father'" (Gal. 4:6).

Thus, you now have the desire (new nature) and the power (indwelling Holy Spirit) to live for God. You are positionally changed from being in Adam to now being in Christ, and experientially changed because the inner transformation of regeneration and salvation begins the process of progressive sanctification, which ultimately leads to glorification.

"For it is God who works in you both to will and to do for His good pleasure" (Phil. 2:13).

While we still have an old sin nature though Satan is opposing us every step of the way, we must grow in the grace and knowledge of the Lord Jesus. It is also true that our entire life is different! If we are what we've always been, we are not saved. I know that I am saved because on the seventh of May, 1974, I received the Lord Jesus Christ as my Savior and also because I have never gotten over it! And it is not that we are trying to be saved. If I asked you, "Are you an elephant?" You would not say, "Well, I'm trying to be!" You either are an elephant or you're not. No one who is trying to be saved understands salvation. *You are either saved or you're not!* You are saved because you have had a personal, life-changing encounter with the Lord Jesus Christ at a point in time. It is a matter of trusting not trying.

So Are You Ready to Be Saved?

If this is something you want to do, then here is a suggested prayer; the words are not what's important but what's in your heart. If God is dealing with you, then cry out to Him:

Lord Jesus, I need you. Thank you for dying on the cross for my sins. I cannot save myself. I cannot even help you save me. But the best I know how, I confess that I am a sinner and believe that the Lord Jesus Christ died on the cross for my sins and rose from the dead. I open the door of my life and receive you right now as my Savior. Come in and make me the kind of person you want me to be.

If you just received the Lord Jesus Christ as your Savior, then you are saved! This promise is based on the authority of God's Word.

"But as many as received Him, to them He gave the right to become children of God, to those who believe in His name" (John 1:12).

A list of my other books: Go to Amazon.com and type in Johnny A Palmer Jr.

Genesis: Roots of the Nation Vol. 1

Genesis: Roots of the Nation Vol. 2
Genesis: Roots of the Nation Vol. 3
Exodus: Redemption of the Nation. Vol. 1
Exodus: Redemption of the Nation. Vol. 2
Book of Leviticus
Book of Judges
First Samuel
Second Samuel
Book of Job
The Gospel of Mark: the servant.
The Gospel of Luke Vol. 1
The Gospel of Luke Vol. 2
The Gospel of Luke Vol. 3
The Gospel of Luke Vol. 4
The Book of Acts
Ephesians: A Manual for Survival
Jude: Hey Jude
Revelation: The Revelation of Jesus Christ
A Manual for Revival
Practical Principles for Studying the Bible
Read Limit 30 mph
Proclamations from a Politically Incorrect Prophet
Elvis Wellness
Awake for the Dawn is About to Break
Rewards of Rejecting Christ
Which Messiah will you Meet?
GPS-23
Spiritual Survivor Man
A Father's Day Message
A Mother's Day Message
I'm For Life
Double Solitaire with the Trinity
Fuel – The Lord's Prayer

Practical Principles for Bible Study
The God of the Second Chance
God who is Good and Angry

Made in the USA
Lexington, KY
12 March 2018